More Praise f

"*Crooked Letter i* is not a loud book. It doesn't rant or rave. It makes no arguments, proffers no manifestos. Instead, the diverse voices represented here achieve something much more astonishing: they sing together; they harmonize. Much LGBT literature, as Stephanie Woolley-Larrea notes, focuses more on coming out than on what comes after. But this anthology plumbs the before, during, and after of that complex process with artful nuance and ruminative grace."

— JULIE MARIE WADE, *Wishbone: A Memoir in Fractures*

"In this meticulously curated volume the regional quickly becomes universal and what was once private, and sometimes painful, becomes, in the telling, something to share and to celebrate. A wonderful addition to the literature of self-discovery and emancipation."

— MADELEINE BLAIS, *In These Girls, Hope Is a Muscle*

"'I was always aware there were boundaries. I just didn't know quite where they were' sums up the experience of growing up gay in the South as described in *Crooked Letter i*. These beautiful stories are poignant and sad, yet life-affirming, and anyone who came out as a young Southerner will closely identify with the peculiarities of this region, like boys having watermelon at a funeral in July or a lesbian drinking sweet iced tea at a lunch counter. Most telling are the struggles to reconcile the Southern incongruencies—a loving God who condemns his children to hell for loving another person—and a feeling that the only place we can call home will never completely be our home."

— RICH MERRITT, *Secrets of a Gay Marine Porn Star*

"*Crooked Letter i* proves that no matter how far gay rights have advanced, the coming-out story is that extra step in the coming-of-age journey that all LGBTQI must take. The collection also proves that Southerners and storytelling go together like Gertrude Stein and Alice B. Toklas. Find a front porch and a glass of iced tea and sit a spell with the stories in *Crooked Letter i*. They will surprise, amuse, move, and devastate."

— JAMIE BRICKHOUSE, *Dangerous When Wet: A Memoir*

"From the sorority houses of Alabama to Florida beaches, from witch hunts to warm embraces, the accounts of these LGBT Southerners provide readers with countless examples of courage and confrontation, with some comic touches along the way. Memorable stories of awakenings blend with powerful images of homecomings: when she returns as a he, when a widower comes out to discover his wife was gay as well, when individuals find themselves both at home and in exile. These gay, lesbian, and transgender autobiographical voices within *Crooked Letter i* provide indelible insight for understanding identity, gender, and sexuality within the American South."

— CATHERINE CLINTON, *Mrs. Lincoln: A Life*

"*Crooked Letter i* affirms everything that is true about the experience of coming out for Southern queers. That is, coming out is an experience that is multiple, thrilling, dangerous, and absolutely life affirming. And 'the South' is multiple, thrilling, dangerous, and absolutely life affirming as well, especially for those of us who call it home. Queer Southern folk of nearly every ilk will hear the hymnal echoes of their own experience in this wonderful collection of voices."

— TERESA STORES, *Getting to the Point*

Crooked Letter i

Crooked Letter

CONNIE GRIFFIN   EDITOR

FOREWORD BY   DOROTHY ALLISON

CONTRIBUTORS

SUSAN L. BENTON   ELIZABETH CRAVEN
LOUIE CREW   CHRISTINA HOLZHAUSER
JACK   LOGAN KNIGHT
THOM KOCH   SUZANNE LEA
ED MADDEN   JEFF MANN
MERRIL MUSHROOM   B. ANDREW PLANT
BETH RICHARDS   VICKIE L. SPRAY
JAMES VILLANUEVA   STEPHANIE WOOLLEY-LARREA

How do you spell Mississippi?
"M - i - crooked letter - crooked letter - i
crooked letter - crooked letter - i
humpback - humpback - i."
And that's how you spell Mississippi!

i

Coming Out
in the South

NEWSOUTH BOOKS

Montgomery

NewSouth Books
105 S. Court Street
Montgomery, AL 36104

Publisher's Cataloging-in-Publication data

Crooked letter i : coming out in the South / Connie Griffin, editor ;
with a foreword by Dorothy Allison.
p. cm.

ISBN 978-1-58838-313-6 (paperback)
ISBN 978-1-60306-362-3 (ebook)

1. Southern states—Coming out (Sexual orientation)—Essays. I. Title.

2015948356

Design by Randall Williams
Printed in the United States of America
by Edwards Brothers Malloy

ACKNOWLEDGMENT OF PERMISSIONS

Grateful acknowledgment is expressed to the following for permission to
publish:

"Southern (LGBT) Living" first appeared in *Binding the God: Ursine
Essays from the Mountain South* (2010) and is reprinted with permission
from Bear Bones Books/Lethe Press.

An earlier version of "Calling" was published in *The Emergence of Man
into the 21st Century*, a collection of essays about masculinity, edited by
Patricia Munhall, Ed Madden, and Virginia Fitzsimons (Jones & Bartlett
with the National League of Nursing, 2002).

Contents

Foreword

= Dorothy Allison =

When I was a girl I understood that my life, my true life, what I really thought about, dreamed and hoped for—all that was a secret, indeed had to be a secret. I feared most of all losing my mother's love, or of shaming her, or even adding to the difficulty of her life by telling her something that would frighten her or make her see me as more endangered than I was.

The larger world outside my somewhat embattled family was another thing altogether. I feared it, of course. I knew that my family in particular was held in contempt for being poor, disreputable, and minorly famous for uncles who occasionally went to jail but more frequently simply engaged in acts of public drunkenness or sudden unexplained violence—mostly visited on other members of my family. Then there were all my female cousins and aunts notorious for invariably arriving at their own weddings with bellies swollen with the babies that would arrive shortly after their minimal honeymoons. We were the disreputable poor, rednecks with bad attitude, crooked by definition, outlaws by declaration. Even I, the high-achieving "good" student hid a caustic attitude behind my relatively respectable demeanor. But that was a secret like almost everything important about me.

When I was twenty, away at college full of hope and terror, I confronted the fact that if I revealed too much about my real life, my stepfather's sexual and physical abuse, or my deep attraction to other young women, I could lose the life I was trying to build. I could be cast out—literally expelled from college or sent off to a mental institution. I had seen another young woman, a gender outcast who so far as I could tell was not really a lesbian, but dressed like one and was in continual revolt against the gender expectations for young women at our nominally Presbyterian private college. Her family appeared in the middle of the night to arrange to have her taken away by force to a facility where, it was expected, she would be fixed.

How would she be fixed? I dreaded the answer to that question and learned with great terror that she had been subjected to electric shock therapy, insulin injections, and continual meetings with determined therapists who led her to renounce all she had been and become what the family wanted her to be. She reappeared a year later, a shadow of whom she had been, head down and hands trembling. She had been vibrant, outspoken, whip-smart, and fearless. This new version of that girl was none of those things and she did not remain long in the dorm, disappearing on another terrible night after trying to take her own life.

I remember thinking that it was all terrible. I left my dorm and climbed up on the roof of the library. I stayed up there all night worrying and grieving. I had barely known that girl but I had known her all too well—her anger and her hopes.

She thought her life was her own.

I had never truly believed that. I had always known I was in some terrible way property—that I belonged to my family in both wonderful ways and terrible ones. My mother's hopes and dreams for me were as heavy as my stepfather's contempt and lust. I was the one who escaped, but who really escapes? Would someone come for me in the night? Would my tentative feminism and carefully concealed lesbian desires doom me before I had done anything I hoped to do?

In this new wondrous age with Supreme Court decisions affirming gay and lesbian marriages, and gender being redefined as nowhere near as rigid as it has previously been defined, I sometimes wonder if anyone knows what our lives were like at the time when I was a young woman, trying to figure out how to live my life honestly in the face of so much hatred and danger. Who are we if we cannot speak truthfully about our lives?

How did we come to this new age in which we can take our lovers home or to church or walk hand in hand down the street without lies or pretense or a carefully crafted fictional stance to protect us?

Speaking truth to power was a tenet of the early women's movement. We would change the world by the simple act of declaring our truth and refusing to back down or lie no matter how virulent the response.

How virulent was the response? Take a look at some of the essays in this book and you will see. But more importantly, you will see the internal evolution of people who wanted simply to be themselves. It was not easy or simple or even a matter of confronting prejudice. Most of these people's deepest struggles were with themselves, their families, and their faith, their most personal convictions.

Confronting the enforced silence of manners and social expectations, we claimed our lives for ourselves. Was it heroic? Was it audacious, marvelous, scary and day by day painful? Of course. Did we change the world? Look around you and marvel.

DOROTHY ALLISON grew up in Greenville, South Carolina. Her novel *Bastard Out of Carolina* (1992), which became a national bestseller, was a finalist for the National Book Award.

Introduction

≡ CONNIE GRIFFIN ≡

The title of this collection, *Crooked Letter i*, derives from the chant that many Southerners will recall learning as youngsters as an aid to spelling that most difficult of states, Mississippi. Like the "S"—the "crooked letter"—we were considered the "crooked" ones in our families, schools, churches, and communities. We believe that having survived as outsiders entitles us to take back the chant, as we have taken back so many other epithets thrown our way over the years. Having earned the right to embrace our "crookedness," we celebrate it—no straightening out needed!

Crooked Letter i: Coming Out in the South is a collection of first-person narratives by lesbian, gay, transgender, and queer-identified individuals who grew up and came out in the South. (I also sought submissions addressing bisexual Southern lives, but unfortunately received none. And I am saddened that the only account from an African American perspective is Louie Crew's piece, telling the story of his partner, Ernest Clay.) The experiences represented here pivot around a central theme—finally finding language to express unnamed feelings, and then discovering, contrary to what we had always thought, we were never the only ones. Revealing a vibrant cross-section of Southerners, the writers of these narratives have in common the experience of being Southern and different, but determined against all odds.

A common theme that runs through these narratives is the lack of role models and language to assist the contributors when their sexual identity came into question. Most had absolutely no one to turn to for their questioning selves; they only learned that there are words for who they are from others' derogatory name-calling or fists in the face, an awakening that proved to be as educational as it was painful. Amidst the recounting of hurtful and hateful experiences, though, these individuals have found many acts of love and acceptance, generosity and understanding, joy and celebration.

ALTHOUGH COMING OUT TENDS to be viewed by the general public as a one-time flash of recognition—an "aha" and "tell"—kind of experience—far more common is a complex kaleidoscope of disruptively confusing feelings revealing a gradual, often reluctant realization of one's difference. Once understood internally, this knowledge is held by many as a deeply guarded secret for years, which can result in a range of socio-psychological consequences. While the realization that one is attracted to the "wrong" gender is deeply personal—a uniquely individual journey—subsequent stages of coming out are often even more daunting. Going public is to look into the face of another—a beloved, a stranger, colleague, neighbor, friend, family member— and *tell* that individual something so private it resonates from the very core of one's sense of self, even as one has no idea how that person is going to respond.

While *telling* is an act of hope and trust and openness, it may mark the end of a relationship, familial and community acceptance, a job, religious affiliation. Still, many muster the courage and do tell. But, then there is another to tell. And then, another . . . Not because LGBTQ individuals are proselytizing or flaunting, as the conservative reaction argues, but because our daily lives necessitate the sharing. "My partner, she . . ." or, "my partner, he . . ." are phrases that implicate our personal choices and have consequences for our lives. Straight people refer to children and husbands and wives and boyfriends and girlfriends, and births and deaths, sickness and health with little thought to the implications of such sharing. For LGBTQ individuals, each sharing can be highly charged from the moment the personal pronoun is used.

So it goes for a lifetime of decisive moments: one must choose to tell—or not. As LGBTQ people everywhere understand, coming out is a narrative spoken within a cultural context of presumed heterosexuality. For the gay, lesbian, or transgendered individual, sexual orientation and/or gender identity flit around the edges of *any* conversation, anticipating self-revelation in something as simple as a question from a coworker about your weekend plans. Some dismiss coming

Editor CONNIE GRIFFIN's Southern roots go back for generations in Alabama, Georgia, and Mississippi. She left the South and relocated to New England in her late twenties for graduate studies in multicultural literature of the Americas. A senior lecturer at the University Without Walls, University of  Massachusetts Amherst, her 2009 book, *To Tell the Truth: Practice and Craft in Narrative Nonfiction*, draws on her years of teaching creative nonfiction writing and American multicultural literature. Connie received her BA from the University of Tulsa, MA from Boston College, and PhD from the University of Massachusetts Amherst. She lives in western Massachusetts with her life partner.

Shurong Wang

out as passé, think that homophobia is no longer with us, ask "why can't we all just relax and be ourselves; who needs labels, anyway," or say "I don't want to know that; it's private." For them, these stories are a poignant reminder that, alas, that world where we will all coexist with tolerance, if not acceptance, around our differences still dwells in some hoped-for future, albeit one well worth working toward.

At this point in history, with recent publicized cases of bullying and suicides on college campuses and in schools, positive cultural visibility is crucial. Studies and polls have shown that families and communities with *openly* gay members, those who have gay friends, or know someone who is gay, tend to hold more accepting positions. The courageous step of sharing one's personal story, an act at the heart of cultural visibility and engagement, is a powerful way to shatter the silence within which so many live.

As someone who did not fully understand the complexity of my own sexuality until after leaving the South, I identify in varied and specific ways with each story shared here. Moving East, going to graduate school and engaging in the study of literature and culture, meeting open-minded, progressive people, I gained an understanding of how personal the political really is, and this freed me to explore my self and my sexuality more fully. May this book do the same for others. The courageous, creative essayists and I offer these narratives in the spirit of lighting the darkness of cultural invisibility.

SOUTHERN LITERATURE HAS WITHIN its ranks a fairly extensive list of gay and lesbian authors, although it is the Southern, and not the sexual, identity that tends to be the focus. Discussion of writers' sexual orientation or gender identity is typically relegated to gay and lesbian, women's, gender or queer studies.

This collection of essays offers a focus on both aspects of identity—Southern *and* sexual orientation or gender identity.

In my research I found another tendency—that of segregating gay from lesbian literature and studies, and transgendered from both gay and lesbian collections. For many good reasons, the majority of LGBTQ anthologies focus on a specific demographic of gay men, *or* lesbian women, bisexual *or* transgendered people. While important to social movements and in creating community, this has also created a lack of contemporary collections representing the diversity of experiences across the LGBTQ spectrum. The thematic focus of *Crooked Letter i* helps fill this void with a diverse range of voices addressing the distinct nature of discovering one's sexual and gender identity *within* the specific regional culture of the U.S. South.

A seismic shift is taking place in the cultural geography of the United States. And even Southern LGBTQ-identified individuals are discovering they have allies who may be "straight, but not narrow," as yet another maxim so concisely states. The Old South has also given way to more nuanced and pluralistic sociopolitical and legal debates on questions of family and marriage rights. We saw the repeal in 2011 of the "Don't Ask, Don't Tell" policy that barred openly gay, lesbian, or bisexual persons from serving in the U.S. armed forces. Then Section 3 of the Defense of Marriage Act (DOMA) was declared unconstitutional in a 2013 ruling that legally married same-sex couples could receive federal protections like social security, veterans' benefits, health insurance, and retirement savings. More recently, the 2015 U.S. Supreme Court decision in *Obergefell v. Hodges* guarantees the fundamental right of same-sex couples to marry nationwide. *Crooked Letter i* participates in these national conversations about inclusion, difference, and diversity. Its themes are grounded in self-discovery, discernment, and the courage to give voice to deeply personal, but highly politicized representations of identity. The first-person narratives presented here illustrate those first courageous steps and beyond as individuals began the journey of living more openly and with high self-regard, often despite others' negative views.

There is the adolescent girl who refuses to surrender her soul to Jesus because she is not yet certain of her own beliefs. There is Logan, who left his hometown as a girl and returned as a young man, hesitant, but hopeful for his grandmother's love. There is Thom, the retired Appalachian teacher who, following the death of his wife and a long and happy marriage, decides it's time to tell not only his family, but also his church community. Jeff, a well-mannered Southern gentleman, his horizons broadened by *Southern Living*, hopes his blueberries and biscuits will help ease the awkwardness of coming out to his ninety-one-year-old neighbor whose company he enjoys. There is Beth who, in her own words, discovers: "If puberty is hell for straight kids, it's something like hell with double-crooked road maps for those who aren't." Jack comes to understand the intersection of race, class, and gender and their implications for one's "place" in the world, while Christina's love of Bible stories, parables, and the antiquated language of biblical scripture is misunderstood as a "calling" from God. There is the girl who discovers that so many others knew before she did. There are those who always knew and those who had no idea. There are the sorority purges following being "outed" against one's wishes. There is the bonfire of burned love letters and the one letter missed, resulting in tragic familial consequences. There is the terrified college student who lied and fled from her college following interrogations and threats of expulsion by the now infamous Johns Committee. There are those who survived the bar raids, strip searches, arrests and beatings.

But, there are also the first kiss, the first touch, the first time; there is first love.

The essays in this collection are as varied and complex as the lives they represent, and for some of the contributors, this is the first time their experiences are being shared publicly. The narratives express a range of emotions about the coming out experience—from genuine perplexity to absolute delight, from shame and self-hatred to relief and joy, from compartmentalization to integration and to integrity.

There is no easy structural codification of the collected stories, and I chose not to impose one. Better to juxtapose for diversity and thematic resonance, inviting readers to come to them in any order. Whether the reader reads through the essays chronologically, moves among them randomly, or through personal selectivity, the thematic threads are there to be found: the dawning of self awareness, the sharing of that awareness, the integration of this aspect of the self into one's life as lived.

STORYTELLING HAS BEEN A Southern tradition for generations, and it is to the story that our essayists have turned to make sense of their sexual awakenings, gender identity, and experiences of love. Like Southern literature more generally, these nonfiction narratives offer regional cadences and linguistic nuances. Unique colloquialisms, speech patterns, and metaphorical imagery add to the power of Southern narrative and will appeal to born and bred Southerners, Southern transplants, expatriates, or those just learning more about the literature of the South. Southern writers can make us smile, cringe, laugh, and cry—all within a phrase or a paragraph. One thing is certain, after reading about the region from the various vantage points offered here, readers will never look at the South quite the same as before.

1.

Almost Heaven

⇒ Elizabeth Craven ⇐

"I think I'm going to keep mine."

Heads around the campfire turned in disbelief. This evangelical youth camp ritual was set in stone. At the end of the day of Christian fellowship a campfire was lit. Then, in the chilly evening air, after a suitable sermon outlining the joys of heaven and the flames of hell, everyone was handed a stick, which represented our souls; born with a sinful nature, we were unworthy to see God. The next few minutes would seal our eternal destinations forever. As the flames of the campfire crackled, we were urged, begged, and cajoled to throw our sticks into the fire—to surrender our souls to Jesus's love and watch our sinful selves burn up in his righteousness. No one ever lasted through all four verses. The guitar strummed the familiar hymns and everyone got up to go to the stone-encircled flames. We all knew the drill. Most of the kids in our Southern Baptist church had done this dozens of times at retreats and summer Bible camps. It was a staple of growing up "churched."

This was supposed to be so easy, so routine. Mumble a few words of "Thank you, Jesus," throw the stick in the fire, and then the all-night slumber party could begin. Who was this girl stopping the show?

"Julia," the minister quietly addressed her, "why won't you

give your life to Jesus who died on a cross to save you from your sins?"

She lifted her head and looked at all of us, the flames circling behind her. "I'm not sure I believe it," she said simply and walked away.

Who was this wonder who could risk the chance of sudden death by lightning, or a falling meteor? Even a snakebite could occur at any moment out here in the woods and she would go straight to hell! What if the church bus plunged off the side of the Cumberland Mountains on the way back? I was in awe, although horrified. Her blood would be on our hands. What would Jesus say if all of us gathered here came to heaven

ELIZABETH CRAVEN is an out and about lesbian who loves the Cumberland Mountains, Uncle Dave Macon Days, and Southern cooking, even though she now lives above the Mason-Dixon Line. She graduated from Tennessee Technological University and Princeton University with degrees in history. At Princeton, she delivered the first gay rights speech by a lesbian student. In St. Louis she wrote a monthly magazine column, *LesTalk*. Elizabeth has worked as a college instructor, community organizer, and professional news clip reader. She makes her living in information technology and shares her life in St. Louis with S. Paige Canfield, another Tennessean. "Almost Heaven" is written for and dedicated to Ann Velasco—"she who listens."

Elizabeth, then and now

except for this one lost soul? Would he turn those sad blue eyes toward me and ask why I had failed him? But if I brought her to the Lord, we would enter heaven together. Her soul would be a jewel in my crown and I could proudly lay it at his feet.

My mind was made up. Who better to lead this Julia to the Lord than me? After all, it was well known that I had memorized more Bible verses that anyone else in the youth group. I was the best Bible scholar, the one most interested in moral purity, and the best public speaker of all the girls. Even though it was generally frowned upon, my youth and zeal had allowed my church to overlook my gender and permit me to speak in the pulpit—not give a sermon, understandably, but still speak on the subject of God's love one Sunday evening. Everyone had told me my speech was a great blessing. I just knew that with God's help, I could touch Julia's heart and bring her to the Lord.

My hopes of a quick conquest were quickly dashed, however. A group of pajama-clad girls, all eager to share their faith and win her soul, had already crowded around Julia. I knew the pack would not disperse until a weary albeit unrepentant Julia declared she wanted to go to sleep. I bided my time.

The next day, I managed to ask Julia if she wanted to go to on a walk in the park away from the relentless witnessing. As much as I wanted to win her to Christ, I found myself impressed by her lack of concern about other people's opinions. Together we walked in the woods and talked. I found myself looking at her hazel eyes, her brown hair, and wondering if I would be allowed to know this rather exotic creature better. She assured me that she really had plenty of friends and that a continuation of our friendship was unlikely. Once again, I was utterly charmed by her disregard.

IT WOULD BE MONTHS before I saw her again. I was in junior

high and she was a grade ahead and already in high school, so there was little opportunity for chance encounters. And then an announcement was made at church one Sunday; there would be a baptism that evening. To my surprise, the person being baptized was Julia. She had finally decided to surrender her heart to Jesus and she wanted to be immersed in the church's healing baptismal waters. I was pleased for her eternal salvation but a little disappointed that I hadn't been the one to bring her to the Lord. Still, it was good that Julia had given in to the overwhelming pressure to believe, wasn't it?

That night we reconnected. She asked me to wait for her in the little room where wet new Christians dried off after the event. There I met her best friend, Kathy, and then she pointed out her mother and brother sitting in the front pew. After that night I would never see them in the church again. Julia asked for my phone number. She said there was so much she wanted to discuss about her new life. I gave it gladly.

In the next few months, I received a number of welcome phone calls. Julia told me she had discovered that I was "that Beth," the one known for winning all the medals during Achievement Award Day. Also, the one known for preaching to the football players about the dangers of smoking during gym class. I pled guilty. Through our conversations, I discovered that she was "that Julia," the one whose father owned a furniture company and who lived in one of the grandest houses on one of the two best streets in town. She admitted she was. In a town of ten thousand, social class had divided us as cleanly as if we lived on different planets.

I found myself hoping our friendship would grow stronger when I began high school that fall. We finally would be going to the same school. At least we might see each other at lunch. Toward the end of the summer, Julia called and asked if I was going to a slumber party hosted by a girl we both knew from church. I had been asked but I rarely went in for socials, preferring books to people in most cases. But if Julia was going, I was going too, much to my parents' amazement.

The night of the party, I found myself strangely jealous when others occupied Julia's attention. I felt restless and uneasy. At the end of the evening as we sat on the floor, she told me to lie down and put my head in her lap because there was something she wanted to tell me. She didn't want the others to hear. Surrounded by girls in little groups talking to each other, Julia encircled my head with her hands, closed my eyes and gently began to massage my eyelids.

Julia chatted, "A boy did this to me the other night. I really liked it, but if you don't relax I'm going to stop. You're as stiff as a board!"

Truth was, I was terrified . . . terrified, horrified, delighted. Nothing had ever felt like this.

Julia leaned close and whispered, "There's something I need to tell you. My parents are sending me to a private girls' school in Kentucky. I'm leaving next week."

My body betrayed me. I started trembling and jerked myself up off her lap.

"Beth, what's wrong? Oh, don't worry. We'll write and see each other during school breaks and holidays. Silly."

I nodded. It was all I could do.

I tried not to think about that night in the coming weeks. Julia left, but true to her promise, she wrote. And I wrote back. As she shared her unhappiness with school life, home, and relationships in letters, I read. I listened. I cared. I found I cared more about her travails than I did my own. Each time she came home, she would tell me my ranking on her Call List (she ranked all the people she wanted to talk to during her visit home). The first time I was fifteenth. At her next visit I had risen to eighth place.

OF COURSE, LIFE WENT on. My quest for grade perfection occupied much of my time. My older brother had found a girlfriend, which sent my family into crisis. My mother was not going to accept a rival for her son's affections lightly. And my lack of social skills had caused unfavorable comment. To satisfy my parents and the church gossips, I found a suitor. He wanted to be a mortician, he was a senior, and my mother liked his mother. We sat in church together. Once or twice, we held hands. At Mother's insistence, I cooked him dinner. He gave me a sandalwood incense burner. I discovered two things: moral purity was easy and I didn't like the smell of sandalwood. After a suitable period, he broke up with me. I returned the sandal-wood incense burner. He thought I was hurt. Even exchange.

One Saturday night, Julia's mother called. She asked me to phone her daughter and talk her into staying in school for the remainder of the semester. Thinking I would be a good influence, she offered to pay for the long-distance call. When Julia answered, she cried. She hated being in a girls' school, she hated the teachers, she was homesick. I asked her if the things that made leaving home a good idea had changed. They had not. After four hours, Julia laughed. The phone bill was so high she now had to stay to justify the cost. I laughed, and I told her I missed her. She told me she knew.

That summer, now 1971, Julia came home for the full three months. She was sixteen and loved to date. I was fifteen and supposedly still in recovery from my first breakup with the would-be undertaker. My brother's relationship was looking serious. While all eyes were on him, my activities were under less scrutiny. Julia and I would hang out with her friends. A few were into the Jesus movement. One night we had a foot washing at Julia's house to celebrate our love of Jesus and our love of each other. My brother picked me up and asked what we were doing. I tried to explain. He thought I and my rich hippie friends were weird. It didn't matter. Julia left again.

By the time Thanksgiving came around, I had finally made it to number one on Julia's Call List. She told me she was feeling guilty that Kathy, her best friend, was now number two. But I was finally number one. I was pleased and confused. If Kathy was her best friend, what was I?

I didn't really want to think about it. For the first time in my life, I had a place outside my head that I wanted to be. Julia and Kathy both loved to lie on their beds with friends, light candles and listen to music—Aaron Copland's "Appalachian Spring," Cat Stevens's "Wild Woman," Carole King's "Tapestry." My life had a soundtrack. And aromas. Julia decided that she was best expressed in the scent of "Jungle Gardenia," a musky perfume whose fragrance hit you long before you were in the presence of the body that wore it. "Jungle Gardenia" lingered in Julia's room, on her clothes, in her hair.

Somehow I had opened a door into a world of sounds and tastes and smells that were not my own. And the touching. Much about Julia was feline in nature. She loved to be petted, stroked, massaged. She would ask to be held. I was appalled at the freedom from convention, and enchanted. A stiff but willing pupil, eager to be shown how to please. But always I was aware that there were boundaries. I just didn't know where they were, for these were entirely new experiences and words just made it all more confusing.

AT LONG LAST CHRISTMAS vacation rolled around. Julia called when she got to town and invited me to a party at her house.

We would string popcorn and cranberries and decorate her Christmas tree. It would be a great way for her to see everyone on her Call List at once. She offhandedly mentioned that she might have a boyfriend there that she wanted me to meet. They hadn't gone out yet but her brother thought it would be a good match. She was looking forward to spending time with him. All those months with only girls were wearing on her. She was ready for some romantic attention.

There was nothing for me to say. I felt shame for how deeply upset I felt.

That night I decided to put the best face on things I could. I would not sulk. I would be the life of the party. When I arrived, everyone was busily at work, laughing, stringing popcorn and pretending to stab each other with the needles. I saw a strange fellow leaning against a door, looking amused and a little bored. I assumed this was the beau. Some were drinking beer and Julia's brothers smelled of pot.

I felt my tension mounting. Julia looked over at me and smiled, a bemused smile. I felt time stand still. Every color, smell, and sound in the room assaulted me. Everything was moving in slow motion. No one could know what I was feeling. I didn't want to know what I was feeling. All I knew was that I would explode if my heart did not stop pounding. I could feel the blood rush to my head. I don't know what was said but I could feel myself starting to blush. I looked at my watch. My brother was coming in fifteen minutes and there was no way I was going to let him come inside and see the beer, smell the pot. I knew there would be hell to pay at home. I needed to get my coat. I needed to go.

Julia had my coat in her hand but she snatched it away. Laughing she ran up the stairs. Without thinking I rushed up after her. I cornered her in the bathroom. Giggling she would hand my coat to me and then snatch it away. I panicked. I had to get the coat and leave before my brother came in. I had to get out of the house before I saw her with him. I had to stop this. I pushed her up against the wall. We both froze.

"Here," she whispered, handing me my coat. "You need to go."

"Yes."

"I'll call you in a few days."

"Okay."

I was shaking as I put on the coat, but I managed to walk down the stairs and get outside. I had no idea what had just happened. I was in shock. Whatever it was, it was raw and dangerous.

There was no one to talk to, and, in any case, what could I say? I didn't even know what had happened. How could I tell anyone about it? What words did I have?

I lived in dread for several days. Finally, she called. The conversation was light, and then it turned to the party. Julia had kissed the boy. It was fun at first but he just wasn't her type. He was not very bright. He wanted to see her again but she had told him no.

It was nothing. She was just curious. She had wanted to know what she would feel about it. It wasn't interesting. I felt myself exhale.

Julia needed to go but before she could hang up she had one more thing she wanted to say. She needed a promise from me. She needed me to agree to hang up the phone as soon as she had said what she needed to say. She didn't want me to say a word. And she didn't want me to call her back. She would call me when she was ready. My heart sank. Whatever it was, it couldn't be good. But what choice did I really have? With an intoxicating mixture of dread and anticipation, I agreed.

"Beth, you're in love with me."

The phone line went dead. After several seconds I slowly placed the receiver on the hook. Then I cried. Tears of joy that my feelings had a name; tears of shame that my feelings were forbidden by every social and religious conviction I had every defended. What a glorious, awful, amazing, sinful torrent of emotions flooded me. When the tears finally subsided, one question burned above all others: what would Julia want to do now?

A few days later, she called. Julia's plans had changed. She and her family were leaving town for the rest of the Christmas break. Would I like to come over for dinner the evening before they left? Her mother and she were trying the Atkins diet so they would be cooking together. They had to leave very early so I could stay over and help pack.

When the day arrived, I found Julia in the kitchen with her mother and father. By the time dinner was finally finished and the packing was done, it was past one in the morning. They were leaving at 4 a.m. to drive to Nashville for their flight. Julia thought it would be best to sleep on the plane so we stayed up.

In the stillness of the early morning in her bedroom, we were finally alone. On impulse I tried to kiss her. She shook her head no. Gently, she explained that we could never do anything about my feelings. I was too strong a Christian and she was too into boys. But she cared about me, very much. She didn't want to hurt me. She took my hand. I started trembling with all the pent-up desire I had never named before. The force of my response surprised her. I pulled away.

Julia looked at me sadly and softly said, "I don't want you to be afraid of me." Then she kissed me. And I responded. Then so did she.

THAT NIGHT WOULD CHANGE the direction of my life forever. Julia and I would struggle with the contradiction of small-town

Southern values and a forbidden lesbian love for the next six years, most of it spent apart. I remained in Cookeville, Tennessee, living at the edge of my beloved Cumberland Mountains, the foothills of the Smokies. She went to school in Wyoming, near the Rockies. We never lived together in Cookeville, except for summers and holidays.

We would write more than four hundred letters to each other and spend a fortune on long distance calls. At seventeen, my closeted relationship with Julia divided my world into two kinds of people—those who knew and those who did not. She and I feared the price openness would exact at home, school, and church. After five and a half years, we decided one day to burn our letters to each other lest someone ever find them. Within six months of that bonfire, our relationship ended. We had, however, missed one letter: it was tucked behind a dresser drawer in my bedroom at my parents' home. When that letter was found by my mother a year later, I was disowned.

The closet door was blown off forever.

2.

Coming Home

⟹ LOGAN KNIGHT ⟸

When I was seven, I laid my head on my grandmother's lap and listened to the church sing—a
collective voice rising beautiful and out of tune.
The soggy heat made my dress itch, made me fidget on the hard
wooden pew. My grandmother closed her eyes and rested her
hand against my ribs, her fingers patting rhythmic beats. She
smelled like powder, and the pages of her Bible mixed musk
and use in the dusty pews. I could feel the vibrations of her
humming, her voice choking a little when she began to cry.

Later, before my grandfather had riled the congregation and
started speaking in tongues—before his face turned red, and
he stomped across the stage—my grandmother leaned close to
my ear, her warm body closing over me, and whispered, "Do
you want some gum?"

I raised up quickly as she dove into her purse, digging between envelopes and pill bottles and old lady mysteries, and
pulled out a blue-green foil wrapper, a particular brand of gum
that had a sweet, gel-mint center. We sat, me swinging my
tiny legs, smiling secretively at one another as we bit into the
gum—the jelly insides bursting in our mouths.

NONE OF US COULD know that the tiny church would be the
last my grandfather would preach in, and as I drive through

Hawkinsville, Georgia, I wonder if I could turn once, then again, and find the Church of God of Prophecy down on Warren Street.

It's August and noon, and the pavement opens up in front of me in huge, gray cracks. Nothing feels heavier than the air, the humidity already wrenching up towards ninety percent. It thickens with every breath until it feels like I'm inhaling steam. Everything around me is fields and tiny houses like my grandmother's, with trash piled around and dead cars in the front yards. When I exhale, the Deep South closes in around me like a heavy blanket that smells like home.

I drive through crossroads with signs pointing to places where my grandfather preached damnation in tiny churches, places where some of the old folks still know our family name, places I cursed and left as soon as I was old enough.

It seems nothing changed in the years that I was gone save for the row of fast-food restaurants. I'm sure my grandmother still reads her Bible every morning and still watches the *Gospel Music Hour* on channel seven every Thursday night.

When I was thirteen, I stood waist-deep in a small pond a few miles outside Newnan, Georgia. The preacher, a short round man, called me into the circle of bodies swaying in the water. I looked back at my grandmother, nodding on the bank, and waded farther in. Dead leaves and muck rolled over my bare feet and floated to the surface. The bodies closed in around me and there was nothing but their voices and the frogs. The man placed a wet hand against my forehead and began to pray. I closed my eyes and imagined the water pouring into my lungs as he held me under until God spoke to him. I imagined drowning. With little warning, the minister pushed against my back and forehead and lowered me under the water. The world was nothing but bubbles and the sun shattering against the surface of the water.

Seconds later, water cascaded down my body, mud in rivulets on my face, and I gulped air. A hand led me towards shore and into my grandmother's arms, my wet body soaking into her.

"That's my girl," she whispered, "you're a child of God now."

BUT, AS I DRIVE through Abbeville years later, I am neither of those things. And that is the story I don't know how to tell my grandmother. I don't know how to tell her that I never found God in her churches. I don't know how to tell her that her granddaughter moved away to bigger cities than she can imagine and became a man. It doesn't work. The narrative of my body is hard to fit into a Southern story.

When I was eighteen, a nurse eyed me nervously before sticking a needle in my arm. She packed cotton around the thin metal and taped it down. I was eighteen, but I looked fourteen. I was eighteen and still too young to have decided this. She read "double mastectomy" on my chart and told me I still had

---

LOGAN KNIGHT was born in LaFayette, Georgia. In 2003, while living in Boston and working on a photo-documentary of drag kings, he attended Gender Crash, a long-running queer open-mic. Fascinated by the diversity of voices and stories he heard, he began attending regularly and eventually signed up for one of the open spots. The overwhelming support of the people he met there inspired him to keep writing. He has since performed his works in venues throughout the U.S. Logan writes about the intersections of family, queer identity, and class. He lives in San Francisco and is pursuing an MFA in fiction writing at San Francisco State.

time to back out. "No one will be mad at you," she told me, in the way that people talk to teenagers. And then the surgeon drew railroad tracks across my breasts, long lines that would be replaced with black stitches like teeth and then, years and year later, thin white scars. He didn't ask if I was ready. Instead, he raised his eyebrow and said, "Last chance."

When they left, I prayed, prayed up to God, my family's God, my God, some God . . . it didn't matter. I finished, and the lights of the operating room crashed into my head. A minute later, I woke up and heard my mother say, "Thank you, Jesus. Thank you, Jesus."

Pulling into my grandmother's driveway, I try to imagine her frail body in her tiny house. The roof is sloping downward now, and the yellow boards are as thin as I remember the skin on her hands. I am ashamed that I have been gone this long. The child that she had last seen, her oldest granddaughter at fifteen, all baggy t-shirts and dirty sneakers, has come back ten years later, a young man in a well-fitted button-down. Would this have been easier if she had seen me during the years testosterone was squaring off my jaw? When my voice broke into shrill squeaks and gravelly dips?

THIS IS WHAT I know, only because I have seen it before. There will be no yelling, no crying; no sermons. If my grandmother cannot reconcile who I am against her religion, if the musculature of my shoulders is an affront to her beliefs, she will simply forget me. She will not speak to me; she will not acknowledge my presence in her house ever again. The sun burns into my arms, and I tense with nervousness.

Every movement of my body towards her door seems heavy. My feet crunch into the hot ground, an inexplicable mix of sand and dirt.

"Who's at the door? Don't stand out there where I can't see you unless you're sellin' something, in which case, don't stand on my porch at all . . . go away. I don't want none."

"It's me, Grandma. It's . . . Logan."

I open the door and the smell of fatback and beans swims into my mouth. An inspirational Jesus winks at me from the wall.

"Hey," she says, as if both greeting me and trying to get my attention. She is laughing in the back of her throat as I cross the room.

"Where've you been?" she asks in the style of Southern matriarchs. Her voice is stern, and she makes it very clear that I have offended her. I can see tears in her eyes, and she holds her arms out for me to hug her. Stooping, I fold my body into hers and tiny arms, stronger than I imagined, pull me tight. I push my nose into her neck. And then there are no words for a long time, her failing eyes focusing and fogging against tears and glaucoma as we survey the landscape of the other's face. The quiet becomes heavy, loaded. I have offended her, but only by my absence. And then she speaks with frankness, like she is telling me nothing I shouldn't already know or find the least bit interesting.

"Your mama told me your new name, but I'm old, child. Us old people have a hard time with things like this." I nod. Her hand traces a line down my cheek and to my chin, and she curls her fingers over to rub my stubble. "You look good, child . . . handsome."

When we finally let go of each other, I watch my grandmother's body, tiny and breakable, move carefully into the kitchen to get us tall glasses of sweet iced tea. She won't hear of any help. And I stare around the room. The walls are a museum of my history; cousins, uncles, groups of children, and fading family portraits. Along the careful rows, there are missing photos with squares of dust surrounding the paint that the frames had hidden. Moving closer, I catalogue faces and names, trying to remember who had been in the now vacant squares.

"I took 'em down," I hear my grandmother say from the door. And then I realize that I am the one missing from the wall, the unconsciousness of skipping over myself.

"I didn't know if you'd be bothered with how you used to look," she says.

In a flash, I see my grandmother, reaching and leaning, treacherously for her, to pull down the pictures of my little girl body in pinafores and faded print dresses.

"The wall looks funny without them," I say. Slowly, she comes to stand beside me, a full head shorter than me, and puts an arm around my waist. Leaning against each other, she nods and says, "Like you're missing from it."

3.

Late News

⇒ Thom Koch ⇐

Ll the "Coming Out" stories I have read were about young people struggling to tell their parents or friends. Mine is different. I came out at sixty-three years old. I had to tell my children that not only was I gay, but my wife of forty-one years—their mother—had been lesbian. And I had to decide whether to come out in a small Southern community.

My wife Sarah and I were an odd couple. Instead of admitting I was gay, I convinced myself that my teenage sexual affair with a neighbor was mere experimentation. My strong feelings for boys had begun when I was thirteen, and by the time I was sixteen the clandestine meetings with a neighbor had become part of my behavior, which was clearly homosexual. My passionate feelings for other guys in high school should have told me the truth, but I latched onto a girlfriend in an effort to be "normal." There was not much tolerance for "queers."

Summertime as a child meant going to the Appalachian Mountains. In my teen years I was accepted as just another kid there. Even as a closeted teenager, I found playmates who accepted my sexual advances. The rest of the year we lived on the edge of the Florida Everglades. While both places were rural, I considered the mountains home and Florida the place for work and school. I felt a sense of pride in my mountain home. Identifying with those young people, somehow I knew

I would live there the rest of my life. As Miami spread out and swallowed my neighborhood, I identified even more with the values of my small mountain town.

I BEGAN MY UNIVERSITY studies at a state school. Correspondence with Sarah, who was four years older and lived in my Florida hometown, had escalated in seriousness to the point where we were considering marriage. Sarah's beautiful philosophy of life matched mine, her love of music and literature excited me, and I fell in love with the chance for a normal life. My mother had told me that sex was a natural part of life, but that marriage should be based on other things. I am not sure what she would have said had I told her that I was not interested in heterosexual sex. Some of Sarah's friends were queer, but I did not discuss my own sexual preference with her until thirty-four years later.

Only once in our marriage did the word "homosexual" come up in reference to both of us. There was a quiz about compatibility in the Sunday newspaper magazine—*Parade*, I think. As we took turns answering the questions, an affirmative came up for both of us on this one: "Have you ever had a homosexual experience?" I looked at Sarah, and she said, "Yes." I marked her column and mine with a check mark. In my mind, I was thinking about the experimental period in my life, during which I was in denial. It didn't register with me that she, too, was homosexual.

Another reason I applied our positive answers in the marriage quiz to myself and not to her was that I had just confessed to having met a guy for a quick sexual exchange. The meeting was a mistake. I thought it was one of my students who called to invite me to his bed. I agreed to go to him, thinking I could talk him out of the dangerous game he was playing. When he turned out not to be a student, but a person hired by the school system, I panicked. Knowing that he could have me fired, I figured the only way to protect myself was to have the same blackmail hold on him. We went to bed. The event was frightening, and my conscience was throbbing. I decided to tell my wife, offering to leave, or let her leave. I was, for the first time in my life, near suicide.

Sarah gently said, "I'm so glad you came back to me." She was wonderful. I could not, and did not, ever violate her trust again.

Our marriage was based on emotional love and consummate friendship. We have two loving, caring sons, and both are good fathers. When asked about our marriage, I can only say that, with the exception of sex, our marriage was nearly perfect. After the first few fights, we realized that we were angry with the rest of the world and not with each other. The fighting ceased. We worked and played together; reading books, gardening, making music.

As far as the sexual part of our relationship was concerned, we both began as heterosexual virgins and had no basis for

THOMAS BRYANT KOCH lives in Raleigh, North Carolina, with his adopted son. He retired after thirty-four years of dedicated service as a teacher. Eschewing total retirement, Thom continued to participate as a poet, composer, and writer in the award-winning alternative education program he created to ensure that underprivileged individuals could earn otherwise unobtainable high school diplomas.

comparison. What we had worked for us, but I was guilt-ridden—to perform with her, I had to imagine being with a man.

At the too-young age of sixty-six, my lifelong love died of cancer. I retired the same year. My time since has been spent writing and composing. I have been fortunate in having a church congregation that allows my music to be performed. My poetry, too, has a limited audience, but my short stories have yet to be published.

WHEN A LONGTIME FRIEND and former piano student of Sarah's visited, I suspected that she was searching for another mate (her husband had died the same year as Sarah), so I told her of my homosexuality. In response, she said that when she was taking lessons years before, Sarah had hit on her; she responded that she was not interested in that sort of relationship.

"*What?*" I asked.

Then I began to open my eyes to many things in our marriage and in her life. About the same time she had opened up to the piano student, Sarah was challenged by a fellow middle-school teacher for "over-comforting" a female choral student. Recall of that "innocent" event now became a revelation. In retrospect, there were numerous times when her relationships with other women were close enough for me to have been a little jealous, but at the time I was not suspicious.

One woman who had worked in the senior citizens' center in Sarah's office had demanded a transfer and in my presence muttered something about "disgusting!" At the time, I thought she was put off by Sarah's use of colorful language. Now I'm not sure. As director for the Council on Aging, most of Sarah's contacts were elderly; Sarah might well have been tempted to make advances to a woman close to her own age.

In an effort to be faithful to my marriage vows, I cautiously avoided serious contacts with men who were attractive to me. Early in our marriage, I was not as cautious about avoiding fast sexual contacts with strangers. During those years shame was my companion.

My behavior was more controlled during three years of military service in Europe as a Russian linguist during the Vietnam War. Under scrutiny of the military, my extracurricular activities were reduced. Both the military routine and the "normality" of a family with children became positive distractions from my "other" life. Our two sons were born during those years, one in California, and one overseas. Sarah lived with me in California but remained with her parents and our firstborn son in Miami while I underwent training in Germany.

There, before the family joined me, I fell in love with a man who was dejected because he had been run out of a small Arkansas town after being exposed as being gay. Now he was being drummed out of the Army for having visited a sex bar. I cried for his situation and for mine. I was determined not to violate my wife's trust by getting involved with this charming, sensitive, hurting human being. I knew that it could not help him or me. However, I did give him one of my rings, which he had greatly admired. He nearly broke my heart when he said I was the only friend he had in the world, but except for a parting hug I never physically touched him.

Two other men tested my willpower with tempting sexual advances, but by then Sarah had joined me, and her presence, as well as the anticipation of our second child, kept my strong natural desires in check.

Our return to Miami in 1965 reintroduced my old haunts and renewed my practice of anonymous partners for quick sexual encounters. Through the years needed to complete my degree and the four years at my first teaching position, I stayed in the closet, but under terrible stress. I was desperate to end my risky behavior.

My parents had been raised in the Deep South, and in 1972 Sarah and I retreated to the same small town in the Appalachian Mountains where I had spent my childhood summers. It was a safe haven for the boys, with the security of everyone knowing everyone, and it was far from the drug-threatened, fume-filled streets of Miami.

I thought it would be easier to control my urges away from a cosmopolitan area. I was, admittedly, seeking a closet and still had no understanding of my dear wife's sexual identity. My extramarital life had become almost nonexistent. Although my eye for men continued, it was under control. Only when I traveled away from home was I tempted to find pleasure.

Looking back, I know the players better: I was gay and she was lesbian, and we were not only happy, we were practically a model couple. We served as co-leaders in Cub Scouts, sang together in the church choir (Sarah was choir director for a time), and shared domestic activities from lawn mowing to childcare. I doubt if it was obvious to the community that our role reversal was nearly complete. When they were sick, the boys came to me for comfort. Though anyone could see Sarah mowing the lawn, they occasionally saw me in that activity, too. No one but I was aware of the hours she spent watching football games and golf tournaments. She was the better chef, but I was the dessert baker. Auto mechanics was her forte—mine was sewing and handicrafts. All the while, I was comfortable in her acceptance of my "motherly" role. I didn't feel that my masculinity was threatened, nor did I ever question her activities and preferences.

EACH SMALL SOUTHERN COMMUNITY has its own personality.

Mine has its share of intolerant rednecks, but there is more tolerance and liberal thinking in Appalachia than meets the eye. Gay couples live peacefully, perhaps because they assimilate quietly. They are not "abrasive" nor do they "flaunt" their lifestyle publicly. They contribute to the local economy. Their anonymity is an exchange for being accepted. Effeminate men and masculine women are regarded as "just that way," as long as there is no proselytizing or efforts at politicizing the community. Some churches are open to same-sex couples; some are not. One openly gay friend told me that he was asked not to join his church. The minister stated that he was a bit homophobic himself. Sadly, I see little possibility for change among fundamentalist religious folk. However, my friend was welcomed into and now attends the Presbyterian Church where I serve as an officer.

After Sarah's death, I decided that I wanted to be out to my family and friends, although I was still not certain that being totally out would be wise in a conservative community. As a retired teacher, my greatest concern was any hurt that might be felt by former students. My church is liberal, and I don't expect my home will be damaged by rock-throwers, but I do not want to hurt anyone, least of all those students whose value systems were in my care.

I came out to my sons by phone. While this was not ideal, they live far enough away (but still in the South) to make personal visits difficult. I explained to them that while I had known my own sexual preference for years, not until after their mother's death had I discovered that she, too, was homosexual. I sympathized with the probable shock but had no apologies for the way I am. I explained that I was not actively involved with another man, and that I was not asking for their permission to be what I am. I reminded them of the deep love shared by their mother, with them and with me, and I made it clear that the family would continue to be love-based from my end. I expressed hope that they would be able to understand that I could not and would not change my sexual preference and that I would be honest about it when asked. I left it to them to decide when their children should know, but said I would be willing to talk to them if asked. I promised full disclosure in answering any questions my sons had.

MY SONS AND THEIR wives accepted my revelations. One of my daughters-in-law said, "Oh, Pop, you can't get rid of us that easily—we still love you!"

One son said he understood it 90 percent. The other son hesitates to talk about it with me but has not rejected me. The oldest grandchild, at sixteen, is not put off by my announcement. He still embraces me when we visit.

I have two brothers, and one is now totally accepting. The other says that I talk about it because I am experimenting with being gay. This is somewhat ironic, for he called me queer throughout our childhood. He may have a slight feeling of guilt. I explained that while I would miss the opportunity to share joy and pain with him, I would not bring up the topic again. I think I embarrass him. I will avoid doing so.

At an evening Bible study of the Sermon on the Mount, the passage, *Blessed are the pure in heart, for they shall see God,* challenged me and I made the difficult decision to tell of my love for a man, but my devotion to a woman. The minister and the adult participants embraced my story and honored my faithfulness. I had thus inadvertently come out to accepting members of my church. Those friends and all others in my community who were told or have discovered my sexual preference have treated me with the same love and respect as always.

Three years after my mate had a soft crossing to the other side, I took in a houseguest for six weeks. He was straight and an artist and self-educated scholar; our conversations were pleasant and stimulating. It was nice to have someone other than my animal friends in the house. I realize that at age sixty-five I would like to find a companion. I do not deny my needs for emotional and sexual closeness that have become, at this point, only topics for poetry, prose, and songs.

I suspect having someone living with me might change the attitudes of some friends and even family. In this area of the mountains, being gay won't matter too much as long as I don't become noisome about it. Being a contributing member of the community will protect me. There are those who love me for who I am and not for whom I prefer to share my life with.

It has been my misfortune to have been most attracted to men in their thirties. They are not interested in a man in his sixties—I can't blame them. One friend in particular has become the male equivalent of my "muse." Each time we visit, I am stimulated to write a song, a poem, or the beginning of a story. A sample:

> *I cannot say how many times*
> *you have not come to me to taste*
> *my tender passion's touch;*
> *the moments when my spirit held its breath;*
> *the hours when pain flowed in to fill the space*
> *left by your absence.*
> *My sanity is saved*
> *by magic memories*
> *that never happened.*
> *My youth is preserved,*

with dreams of meetings
that will never be.

    I have written several short stories and a novella about challenges associated with being gay. Some of my poetry has been inspired by gay friends. My love songs are innocently cloaked to be gender nonspecific, but they have special friends in mind.

    While some of my works are still in the closet, my mind is not. I am no longer ashamed to eye a good-looking man. I look for the day in the near future when, even in this small Appalachian mountain town, I can be totally out.

4.

Southern (LGBT) Living

⇒ JEFF MANN ⇐

For a few years in the early to mid-eighties I was a fan of *Southern Living* magazine. A lesbian friend introduced me to the magazine and gave me a gift subscription. I was single, poor, and hadn't traveled much, so the articles, recipes, and slick photos gave me exciting glimpses into a larger world I had yet to experience. I read eagerly about and dreamed of being in glamorous cities like New Orleans, Savannah, and Charleston. I smacked my lips over pictures of fried chicken, scalloped oysters, coconut cake, and mint juleps, and wished I had a handsome lover with whom to share such Southern delights. For a few Christmases, my mother gave me recipe collections the magazine published annually in book form.

Southern Living was a good way to remind myself of what pleasures the South had to offer. As a gay man who had spent almost all of his life in relatively small towns in Appalachia, I was more than aware of what nastiness my native region contained. Homophobia and Christian fundamentalism were ubiquitous, gay life was sparse. The same love for tradition that I had inherited from the South also encouraged in many of my fellow Southerners reactionary attitudes, prejudice, and a surly suspicion toward anything different. Like Quentin Compson in William Faulkner's *Absalom, Absalom!*, I used to mutter, "I don't hate the South! I don't!" in an attempt to convince myself. Browsing through *Southern Living* was one way to come to terms with my problematically complex identity as a Southern gay man. Staying in the closet was another. My sense of self wasn't sufficiently solid to allow frequent coming out till graduate school.

Only a few months of living in the crowded, noisy, and frantic Washington, D.C., metropolitan area in 1985 convinced me that, as ambivalent as I felt about my small-town rural South, I liked it a hell of a lot more than a big city. I returned home and have lived in West Virginia and Virginia ever since.

I realized I was gay in 1976, so I've been balancing my Southern and gay identities and coming out to people in the South for more than thirty years. By now, *Southern Living* has little to teach me. I've been to those places I used to read wistfully about in its pages. I know how to cook all sorts of tasty Southern food for my partner and friends. But Southern living as an openly gay man? Now that remains interesting, as challenges always are. It's an ongoing education. As a teacher, I know that examining one's own learning process often confirms and affirms that learning, so let me examine this Southern education and share some of the things I've discovered.

I CAN'T REMEMBER WHETHER it was Vince Gill, Billy Ray Cyrus, or Travis Tritt. Some male country-music star. I know it wasn't Tim McGraw; I would have remembered that, since I've been desperately in love with him for many years. I do, however, remember who my fellow concert-goers were that evening at the Roanoke Civic Center and what the pre-concert dinner conversation was like, for it was one of the first times I came out after being hired in 1989 as an English instructor at Virginia Tech.

Tammy and Lori were members of the English Department

staff, Tammy the administrative assistant, Lori the bookkeeper. Both were country-bred like me. Their Virginia home county, Giles, borders my West Virginia home county, Summers, at the state line. Though Virginia Tech is solidly in the Appalachian South, most of my colleagues in the department were far from Southern, so Tammy's and Lori's mountain accents made me feel at home. We shared the same values, loved the same landscapes, grew up on the same food. And we enjoyed country music, often attending concerts together.

Over down-home Southern food in Roanoke's K&W Cafeteria—let's say country-fried steak, peppery milk gravy, mashed potatoes, green beans, corn, and coconut cream pie, since that's

John D. Ross

JEFF MANN grew up in Covington, Virginia, and Hinton, West Virginia, receiving degrees in English and forestry from West Virginia University. His poetry, fiction, and essays have appeared in numerous publications, including *The Spoon River Poetry Review, Prairie Schooner, Shenandoah, Laurel Review, The Gay and Lesbian Review Worldwide, Crab Orchard Review, Arts and Letters,* and *Appalachian Heritage.* He has published three poetry chapbooks, five full-length books of poetry, two collections of personal essays, a volume of memoir and poetry, three novellas, four novels, and two collections of short fiction. He's won two Lambda Literary Awards. Jeff lives in Pulaski, Virginia, and teaches creative writing at Virginia Tech in Blacksburg, Virginia.

what I tend to order at such spots—I came out to them. It was one of those preemptive self-revelations, where a straight person you honestly like starts talking about gays, and in order to save her or him from future embarrassment—since uninformed straight people often say stupid things about gays—you come out. Lori started a sentence about gay men—this many years later, I don't remember the content, but it must have seemed to me potentially negative—so I interrupted, telling Lori and Tammy I was gay. They might have been mildly surprised, but neither seemed truly shocked. There was a second or two of awkwardness, both said that was fine with them, and off we went to the concert. A few days later, Lori even asked me a few simple questions about what gay life is like.

Lori left the department a year or so after that, but Tammy remains. Over the years, we've discussed relationships, shared occasional lunches, talked about departmental politics, *Will and Grace, Brokeback Mountain*, country music, motorcycle runs, homophobia, and down-home cooking. She was one of my major comforters and supporters during my eventually successful bid for tenure, a process made unsettling by the very queer and often erotic nature of my publications.

One winter day when I wrecked my pickup truck in a sudden snowstorm, her husband Lee, a good-looking country-boy trucker, fetched me in his huge four-wheel-drive and they put me up for the night. I made biscuits, Tammy cooked up home-canned beef, and we had a good meal and a few drinks and watched the mountain snows come down. Their hospitality, like that of most Southerners, was superb.

What have I learned from this? One, Southerners tend to like Southerners in the same way that most of us are soothed by sameness and made somewhat uncomfortable by difference. I think that my Southern qualities make my gayness easier for

other Southerners to accept. It helps that I'm friendly, not criti-
cal; mannerly, not abrupt and blunt. Tammy and Lori, neither
of whom had experienced gay people up close before, already
knew and liked me, so they were predisposed to continue liking
me even after my homosexuality was disclosed. What they did
share with me allowed them to accept what we didn't share.
(Well, we don't share heterosexuality, but we do share an ap-
preciation for men. Tammy and I still compare lustful notes
about various sexy country music and film stars.)

Two, I was reminded of the importance of coming out.
Since that evening at the K&W, I've been pretty much out to
everyone in my department. By now—I've taught at Virginia
Tech for almost twenty years and published lots of openly queer
material during that time—I'm well known as the Appalachian/
gay writer, "the Mountaineer Queer," as I half-jokingly describe
myself. One of the many reasons I've insisted on being so open
has to do with stories Tammy has told me since I came out to
her. She has sternly scolded a long series of homophobes about
their attitudes, defending me in particular, or My Queer Kind
in general. Influenced by this liberal attitude, her daughter
Nicole took a persecuted gay kid under her wing during high
school. I suspect that Tammy is naturally understanding and
kind, but I like to think that knowing me has made her even
more likely to spread the word that gay people are just fine
the way they are. My guess is that such grass-roots one-on-
one interactions are more effective political activism than any
marches or rallies. The conservative Highland South needs as
many folks like Tammy as it can get.

I DO IT IN several ways. I used to make a big production about
coming out to my classes, informing students that this personal
disclosure was meant to contribute to their education in ways

that specific course materials could not. Now I do it casually, simply because many of my students, master web-surfers that they are, already know I'm gay. They check out websites that rate teachers and I have a web page, so my homosexuality is likely known to a good number of them on that first day of class in Intro to Creative Writing or Poetry Workshop. Now, instead of a grand announcement, I frequently mention "my partner, John," during the little anecdotes I use to start the class or to provide illustrations for various points I want to make. We Southerners are, after all, supposed to be good storytell- ers, and students have told me in the past that my illustrative tale-telling is one of my best teaching techniques. I mention meals John and I have made, movies we've watched, trips we've taken together. I use our commitment ring as an example when I talk about symbols, and I manage to get in a few caustic words about anti-gay-marriage laws while I'm at it. When I talk about dialect and other distinguishing features of subcultures, I use not only Southern examples—I say "cain't," not "can't"—but gay examples—"Woof!" is what a randy bear says in response to a sexy man. I joke about my crushes on assorted country music stars and actors and even wear one of my several Tim McGraw T-shirts to class when the weather is warm. I confess that the movie *300* must have been made for me, between the classical setting, the half-naked men, the swordplay, and Gerard Butler's black beard. I have no discipline problems (being a burly male is, I know, helpful in this regard), my classes generally go well, most students seem to be relaxed and to enjoy themselves, and I receive high student evaluations of my teaching, enough so to have netted a coveted Certificate of Teaching Excellence from Virginia Tech.

What have I learned from this? True, it's a liberal environ- ment, the university. True, most of my students are somewhat worldly young people from the northern Virginia suburbs. True, I am in charge, so they are less likely to be publicly homophobic. But I think my manner helps. Except in the most virulent queer-hating cases, good will goes a long way. I treat my pupils with respect, I don't put them on the spot, I'm helpful and kind, I'm relaxed, honest, and humorous, and I'm truly concerned about the quality of their classroom experience.

Here, too, I am deliberately out because I want them to know a gay person. I want—with my relatively masculine and fairly Appalachian behavior, dress, and looks, with my bushy beard, bear-brawn, faded jeans, and cowboy boots—to challenge whatever stereotypes and preconceptions they might have about gay men as perpetually effeminate, urbane, delicate, over-refined sophisticates. After a semester with me, I'm hoping that any homophobia they might have possessed will have dwindled a bit, as well as any biases they might have entertained about dumb hillbillies.

I WAS NERVOUS, MOVING to the little mountain town of Pulaski in 2005 after living all those decades in university towns. But the house was super-affordable and remarkable, a solid, brick Georgian home built in 1900 and in immaculate shape, property John and I couldn't resist. He planned to join me as soon as our West Virginia house sold, but meanwhile I was living alone in Pulaski and commuting to Virginia Tech on the days I taught. How, I wondered, would this neighborhood take to an openly gay writer? I was far too old to consider a return to the closet.

Women tend to be easy for me to charm. I've never been a beauty, but I'm not bad looking, and my instinctive Southern politeness and deference win women over fast, especially older women. So I wasn't too worried about my female neighbors. Plus I'm a good cook, and I thought my pies and nut breads might serve nicely as caloric buffers against homophobia.

But Roger was as macho as they come, a good ol' boy of the first variety. I generally get along with good ol' boys, since I have a streak of G.O.B. myself, but I was still a little anxious about how Roger would respond that morning he had me over for coffee and I explained that "my partner John" would be joining me in the house at some point.

Roger didn't miss a beat. Even after he got "the gay thing," he and I got on fine. We had coffee often, ran around in his huge pickup truck, got drunk on bourbon and tequila, smoked cigars under the stars. I wondered sometimes if he would have taken up with me so easily if I were less like me and more like the gay men mass media have encouraged straight folks to expect: thin, witty, fashion-conscious, animated, effete. The interest Roger and I shared in pickup trucks (I envied his), cowboy boots (he coveted mine), motorcycles, and small-town greasy-spoon hot dogs created a kind of good ol' boy bond between us that I can't imagine him sharing with gay men of more discernible stripe. In other words, he didn't care if I were gay as long as I was masculine.

My guess is that this would be true of many "Good Good Ole Boys" (to use Florence King's categorization from her great book, *Southern Ladies and Gentlemen*). The "Bad Good Ole Boys," they're the kind who wouldn't care how butch you are. In their eyes, if you're queer, you're queer and thus "need killin'." They wouldn't care how big you are, either: they travel in packs, so it's always going to be several against one. This is why there's a hunting knife under the seat of my pickup truck.

Roger's acceptance has been mirrored by the attitudes of the various local workers John and I have had into our home for various reasons: the plumber, arborist, driveway paver, electricians, and storm-window crew. All have been country types like myself, but, unlike myself, presumably straight (a few have been disturbingly hot, goateed cubs, but that's another story, one I'll probably write for an erotica anthology one of these days). All have been aware that two men in their forties share this house. Most, I assume, know what that cohabitation means. A few, I'm guessing, have noticed my Tim McGraw calendar hanging on the sunroom wall. Who knows what they say about us after they leave? While in our presence they're as nice as can be, every one of them perfectly polite. They want our business; that's part of it, I know. Part of it's my country-boy camaraderie with them, part of it's a small-town friendliness, part of it's the live-and-let-live attitude that Appalachia possesses more than many regions. Whatever it is, I'm thankful.

PEOPLE SURPRISE YOU. SOME you might imagine to be intolerant turn out to be accepting; some you expect to be accepting turn out to be intolerant.

I call her Mizz Mayberry (as a Southerner, I was not brought up to call my elders by their first names). She's my next-door neighbor. She's ninety-one, frail but sharp, funny, and smart. No one brings out the well-mannered Southern gentleman in me like Mizz Mayberry.

When we first moved in, I took Mr. and Mrs. Mayberry a basket of blueberries I'd picked at a friend's farm, hoping that the gesture might win them over and manufacture some good will I might need in the future. When Mizz Mayberry asked me what church I attended, I started worrying. When I found out that they didn't allow alcohol in the house, I worried more. I assumed that, as old as they were, their attitudes would be rigid, traditionalist, religious, and, well, homophobic. I assumed that they didn't understand the full import of "My partner John will be moving in soon," the phrase that good ol' boy Roger had understood immediately. "Partner" means "business partner" to folks of the Mayberrys' generation, I reasoned. They're going to have a shock when they realize homosexuals live next door, I thought. I prepared myself for chillier interactions once the truth was out. I liked them very much, and I dreaded their judgment and disapproval.

In February 2006, the *Roanoke Times* ran an article about me, "The Brokeback Professor," discussing my book *Loving Mountains, Loving Men* and the elements it shared with *Brokeback Mountain*. A big color photo of me accompanied the article. My residence was listed as Pulaski. In other words, I was suddenly even more identifiably queer than before (and indeed I received, along with many friendly e-mails from fellow LGBT folks, at least one virulent note telling me to "get medical help"). At the same time that I was a bit anxious about coming out in such a public way, the writer in me basked in the ego-food and attention, and the activist in me figured becoming more widely known as the Appalachian gay writer might help other Appalachian queers feel less alone.

I picked up that issue of the *Roanoke Times* early that morning at a nearby gas station, then read over the article at a local coffee shop before returning home. I felt a little exposed, true, but I knew that: one, no one would pay the article much attention, writers being the sort of public figures that few people find interesting; and, two, my usual baseball cap and dark glasses were likely to disguise me from the roving bands of well-armed gay-bashers I was suddenly sure stalked the Pulaski streets.

Mizz Mayberry called me at 10 a.m. When I recognized her voice, I steeled myself for the worst. Instead of expressing horror, disgust, or pious shock, she asked, in her sweet, quavering voice, if I wanted her to save her copy of the newspaper so I might have it for my files. She also congratulated me on the publication of my book and expressed a desire to read it. Since then she has remained a warm and welcoming neighbor. We have reciprocated her kindness, fixing her fence, taking her baked goods, picking up candies amidst our travels to appease her chocolate craving. She owns a signed copy of *Loving Mountains, Loving Men*. One summer day she even hosted a little poetry reading on her porch. Several neighbors attended, and cookies and lemonade were served. I read some of my poems (admittedly avoiding the man-loving-man verse and focusing on the poems about Appalachian living) and played the mountain dulcimer. When her ninety-three-year-old husband passed away, John and I were two of a select few invited to the funeral home for a private service. As I write this, in February 2008, snowdrops are springing up like tiny ivory bells beneath her oak tree. Paradoxically, their evidence of new life in a new year makes me worry about her health and advancing age. I pray that she lives many more years to admire in late winter the snowdrops beneath the oak, then in spring the daffodils on the wooded slope behind her house, then in summer the huge lemony blooms of the magnolia tree in her side yard.

THEN THERE ARE THE unpleasant surprises. John says they were simply drunk, not harassing me deliberately. It could have been anyone's mailbox, he says. I don't know. What I do know is that the closest I've gotten to killing someone occurred not in a small, conservative town like Pulaski but in Blacksburg, the liberal university town where Virginia Tech is located, where I lived for fifteen years.

A group of young people lived across Airport Road from the old house I rented for my last eight years in Blacksburg. They might have been graduate students; I don't know how many actually lived there, or how many were friends who came and went. I like my quiet and privacy, so we had few interactions before the night of the stoning. But those hadn't been particularly pleasant. On two or three occasions I'd gone over to tell them, politely but sternly, that their middle-of-the-night party music and conversation were disturbing my sleep. The young woman who seemed to be the spokesperson always apologized, but it sometimes took two visits in the same night for them to get that I meant business.

It was a night in mid-May 2005, one of the last times I slept in that house. My lease was soon up, and I was to move into the Pulaski house John and I had just bought. John was in Charleston, West Virginia, that night. We owned a house there we were planning to sell, so he continued to work there and we got together on weekends. Thus, I was alone when the noises woke me, a series of dull thumps from somewhere outside. I checked the bedside clock: a little after midnight. I raised a blind and peered out.

Another party was going on across the street. It was a warm evening, and many people were drinking on the front porch, celebrating the semester's end. I had to watch them for a while before I figured out what was causing the intermittent thumping that had woken me. A young man was pelting my mailbox. He stood on the opposite side of Airport Road with a beer in one hand. With the other he picked up rocks and threw them across the street. He had a good arm. He struck the mailbox often.

One of the greatest and most nightmarish fears of many LGBT people is to face or be chased by a violent, hostile heterosexual mob. We move, occasionally invisible, occasionally not, amidst such people all the time. We wonder how they might hate us if they knew what we are, we wonder how cruelly they might treat us if they had that knowledge and the power to implement their disgust. This is no doubt why I always relate to the persecuted monster in horror films: Dr. Frankenstein's creation fleeing the torch-wielding villagers, the vampire hiding from his hunters. This is no doubt why, despite my oft-professed title as "The Only Gay Man in North America Indifferent to Broadway," I loved *Wicked* when John dragged me to a performance during our last trip to New York—it's all about being a harassed, detested, maltreated, maligned outsider. Being LGBT anywhere except in the most liberal setting is bound to create in us a siege mentality, a paranoia that is sometimes reasonable, sometimes not.

I don't know if my response was reasonable. It was more instinctual, I think: the instinct of a threatened animal. I should have called the police; a postal service employee friend of mine has said that I could have gotten them in serious trouble for defacing a mailbox. But I'm nothing if not prideful. My Southern sense of masculine honor insisted that I defend myself rather than involve legal authorities. So I pulled on my jeans, cowboy boots, sweatshirt, cowboy duster, and baseball cap: my usual attire, but, in that context, I was well aware that such butch clothing would help make me more intimidating. Still, one man, however big and angry, isn't much of a match for a crowd, and there was indeed a small crowd of people on that front porch and on that lawn across the street. So I took my own equalizer, albeit one more archaic and romantic than the solid practicality of the firearms many country boys might have toted in similar circumstances.

I grew up on King Arthur's exploits, on *The Iliad*, *The Odyssey*, *The Aeneid*. More recently, I've relished films like *Gladiator*, *The Lord of the Rings* trilogy, and *300*, as much for the sword-swinging action as the sexy bearded men. In other words, I own several knives and swords. It took me a minute or two to choose. Aragorn's ranger sword was far too long to conceal in the pocket of my duster. My Scottish dirk was too long and straight to fit. But Aragorn's elven hunting knife, when removed from its wall plaque, was just right. The scimitar curve of it allowed it to slip into my duster pocket, and it, like all the other blades, was sharp enough to do damage.

My father and sister are both attorneys. I know about the laws prohibiting concealed weapons. I didn't care. I was not going out there unarmed. Again, I don't know whether this move was unreasonable or wise. I do know that, if ever faced with the same situation, I'd do the same thing.

The confrontation didn't last long. Shaking with adrenaline, I strode to the front of my lawn, the top of a small slope overlooking the street, a high point that, I realized, gave me a tactical advantage. With my habitual sarcasm I asked the young man if he was enjoyed his target practice. Between the rage and the fear, my voice wasn't as steady as I wished it had been. I accused him of stoning my mailbox. He denied that he'd been stoning my mailbox. I quipped that I must then be having vision problems since I'd clearly seen him do it, and the young woman I'd dealt with before apologized, promised me that no one meant me any harm, and swore that the party was dispersing. That was it. Not much of a story, I must admit.

The story is in what might have happened. When I turned away from that crowd and stalked back toward my house with a deliberate slowness that I hoped might project the fearlessness I did not feel, I expected one of those stones to hit me between the shoulder blades. If it had, if one of those no-doubt-drunk guys had gotten his dander up and followed me with violence on his mind, I would have pulled that knife. I would never have carried it out there if I hadn't been truly prepared to use it. At the very worst, I would have killed someone. Less terrible possibilities were wounding someone or being arrested for carrying a concealed weapon.

Instead, I sat on my porch in the dark, pulled the knife from my coat and stroked it as the party across the street broke up, people drove away, and lights in the Party House finally went off. The weight and sharpness of the scimitar were a comfort. When everyone was gone, I walked around the property, checking the perimeters, making sure no one had decided to outflank me by sneaking around the back of the house. I was, at this point, operating more like an alert animal or novice soldier than a writer and professor. I stood in the darkness and sniffed the early blooming honeysuckle. I walked down to the mailbox, touched its dented sides, and examined the scattered rocks on the ground around it. Then I returned to my house. I pulled off my boots and turned off the light. I slept still clothed, with Aragorn's elven hunting knife unsheathed on the floor by my bed.

For a long time I wondered, if the mailbox stoning were truly a malicious anti-gay gesture, how those partygoers knew I was gay. As I've said above, I look like just another country boy. I lived there alone. John was only one of a number of people, male and female, who visited me. It was months later that I pieced together facts that helped all this make sense. Living next door to the Party House was a woman who briefly dated a colleague of mine. She told him that she and her friends in the Party House called me "Spooky Guy" because I lived in an old ramshackle house, wore black occasionally, and kept to myself. She was later to write me a letter telling me how much she enjoyed reading my books of poetry. I can only guess that the homoerotic nature of much of those poems was some-thing she shared with her neighbors. Whether those stones were lobbed at a conveniently close mailbox, at the world in general, at my previous complaints about their noise, or at my homosexuality, I will never know. But I do know now that some if not all of the drunken folks at the Party House were aware that I was gay.

THAT TRAUMATIC EVENING HAS been the exception, not the rule. Being Southern, butch, and brawny has made my life in the South much, much easier, I know, than the lives of many LGBT folks. Having patterned myself on the kind of beefy, bearded country boys I desired in my youth, on the surface I have assimilated. No one seeing me drive my pickup truck down the country roads between Virginia Tech and Pulaski or interacting with me superficially at the grocery store or a local restaurant would ever guess that I'm a professor of creative writing who occasionally teaches gay and lesbian literature, as well as a Wiccan, a leather bear, a poet, a bondage enthusiast, a writer of erotic BDSM fiction, a member of Phi Beta Kappa, and a lover of ethnic cuisine, international travel, Greek and Roman literature, Nordic sagas, and Celtic culture. My differences are, in other words, complex, deep, radical, and myriad, but not visually apparent. I look and occasionally act like a Southern redneck, and this saves me from many a conflict, allowing me to conserve my energy for activities more fruitful than regular fisticuffs with homophobes. This is not true for many of my queer kin, and I can only imagine what daily stresses, humiliations, and difficulties they must experience if they remain in the small-town or rural South. I've had enough students tell me stories of name-calling and abuse on the Virginia Tech campus to guess at how hard it is to be discernibly gay. Kids suspected of being queer at the local Pulaski High School are made miserable, I've heard, just as they were made miserable in the high school I attended so long ago in Hinton, West Virginia.

As relatively easy as I've had it, I don't know how many

of my own "Southern Living" experiences might be helpful or relevant to other LGBT Southerners. Certainly my early interest in those glossy photos and articles in *Southern Living* magazine was no preparation for dealing with hostile preachers, "Bad Good Ole Boys," rock-wielding drunks, or my own fear and rage. But that magazine did help confirm in me a lifelong love of the American South, despite its flaws, and that love has helped me remain here. I love the mountains, the pastures, the accents, the good manners, the friendliness and hospitality, the folk culture, and the deep sense of history. On most days, that love is greater than my hate for my native region's weaknesses. On bad days, such as when Virginia passed its law against same-sex marriage, the love beats out the hate just barely. But, don't most of us, gay or straight, Southern or Yankee, both love and hate where we're from?

For some queer folks, the hate they face in the South causes them to hate in return, and what they learn to love is life in the Castro, in Silver Lake, in Chelsea, in Dupont Circle, those gay communities elsewhere. I wish them luck and wish them better lives, queerer lives, in those faraway places far too busy, crowded, and costly for my taste. For those of us from the South who choose to remain, who have some sense of the horrible ache of homesickness, I wish us bourbon, barbeque, and bis-cuits, determined queer comrades and devoted lovers. I wish us the strength that allows life on the front lines, where the battle is fiercest and its outcome unsure, where courage counts for everything, and where the greatest changes can be forged.

5.

The Third Time

⇒ BETH RICHARDS ⇐

I had no idea that I was coming out when, at age eight, I pledged my undying love, proposed marriage, and offered to make a bevy of babies with a really cute girl in my rural northwest Florida Brownie troop. My pronouncement was met with a quizzical look from the Brownie in question and chilled silence from the troop leader. Some of the silence came from disbelief, but I am sure some came from acute discomfort—after all, a well-raised Southern eight-year-old wouldn't think—much less know—about such things, now would she? A few days later, I received a brief, stern talking-to: those things might cause people to think the wrong things about me, and we didn't want that, now did we?

As I listened, I nodded as if I understood, though I was obviously fuzzy about human biology and not a few other realities. Yes, I had observed that men and women got married, and I knew that babies resided in the female belly before they were born. But, it never occurred to me there would be a problem with us both being female. There would be two bellies—maybe we could make twins.

However, I soon came to understand that I had breached a barrier so audacious that no one was willing to correct me in any useful detail. I certainly knew many actions were considered wrong. My family roots were deeply embedded in the Church of Christ, a fundamentalist Southern church, which each Sunday—between Sunday school lessons, Bible verse memorizing, hymns about lost souls wailing through a very hot eternity, and an hour-long "come to Jesus, sinner" sermon—provided a thorough and detailed list of "thou shalt nots."

My parents' list provided additional expectations about the behavior of nice young ladies: not being noisy or rude, not backtalking, not using the Lord's name in vain, no adultery (becoming an adult?), no blasphemy (having a blast?), no picking or poking or pulling at anything between the chest and the knees. As for the "thou shalts," the list included obedience, good grades, looking pleasant rather than "ugly," and deference to elders, no matter how much sweaty, sloppy "shugah" they wanted to hand out after church and during revivals. We were also commanded to love our neighbor, but no one bothered to tell me that love, neighborly or otherwise, did not extend to other Brownies.

Because the Brownie business was never mentioned again, my shame eventually faded. I made A's in school, looked "ugly"

BETH RICHARDS, a northwest Florida native, has lived in Connecticut since 1991. This essay is part of her memoir in progress. She recently earned an MFA in Creative Writing from the Solstice Low-Residency MFA Program at Pine Manor College, and she teaches academic writing and creative nonfiction at the University of Hartford. Her work has appeared in *Fourth Genre, Solstice Literary Magazine: A Magazine of Diverse Voices*, and *EPluribusMedia*. She dedicates this essay to "the keeper," Lilah, who died in May 2013.

as seldom as possible, and memorized more Bible verses than any other child in my class. But I never had a chance to put words to the questions and feelings I carried quietly but uneasily inside. I knew something was different—and transgressive—in me. I also knew that whatever it was meant trouble, so I kept my thoughts and feelings to myself. If no one knew what I was thinking or feeling, then I couldn't inadvertently say those things that would make people think the wrong things of me.

THE SYSTEM WORKED FAIRLY well—until the first rumblings of puberty.

If puberty is hell for straight kids, it's something like hell with double-crooked road maps for those who aren't. The world is steeped in images, music, and stories about what romantic love is—and those images, music, and stories always contain a he and a she. The same explosion of hormones was churning inside me as in every other adolescent, but every surge traveled back roads that led me to other females. Only females.

I could rationalize feelings for some people, like teachers, as infatuation. Almost everyone has had a crush on a teacher, and the gender mismatch never seems to concern anyone. But then I'd find myself in the girls' locker room at school. Or with the girls all crowded into a single beachside hut, skimming off our sweat-soaked shorts and tees and pulling on swim suits for the warm, clear Gulf waters ("it's ok—it's just us girls"). Or in a department store dressing room after a friend invited me in to admire her new, cleavage-revealing shirt: I thought I would die on the spot. Seeing a partially clothed female body was like being hit in midbrain with a flash lightning from a summer thunderstorm, a bolt that traveled down my chest, into my belly, then settled—make that landed, there was nothing settling about it—right between my legs. I pleaded with my brain-chest-belly-crotch to please, please stop. Couldn't they see how the world had been created, from the very beginning of time? Didn't they know God was watching and recording each of my nasty erotic eruptions in the Eternal book? Didn't they understand that I would take the swift, sure four-lane highway into the deepest pits of hell?

At that point, I had never heard the words *lesbian, gay, queer,* or even *homosexual* (especially the latter, given that the syllable *sex* was never uttered in our house). But I knew that whatever I was, it was bad, and—lacking the moral backbone to straighten myself up (I was too ignorant even to appreciate the pun)—I was doomed. Through trial and mostly error, I discovered the best way to reduce the electric surges was to avoid looking at people. I studied my shoes a lot. Kept my nose in a book. Stared at the sky. But no matter how hard I tried I couldn't keep out of my mind the images of the sloped-in waists that flared into curving hips, the gently swaying breasts, or the amazingly varied triangles of hip and pubis. They overran my dreams and I awoke in a sweat, both satiated and terrified, to the reality of my own sickening self.

MY SECOND COMING OUT—ALSO accidental, though in a different way—occurred in eighth grade, when I learned a new word: dyke. It was spat in my direction by a tall, sneering girl in my gym class, right before her balled-up fist landed under my chin. As my head snapped back I saw stars; when she grabbed a chunk of my hair and pushed my head into the locker, I saw more. She was not alone. While she acquainted my head and face with the ventilation grate on the locker, her two companions landed slaps and blows on my kidneys, ears, and upper back. With each blow, they hissed a litany: "Queer, dyke, pervert." The most effective kidney puncher—a tall, quintessential cheerleader-type with round, cornflower blue eyes, pert nose, and waist-length blond hair—took my arm and twisted it behind my back. She pressed her lips to my ear. "If we catch you again, bitch, we'll tear you to pieces."

Had I been looking? Had my guard fallen so far? I had, I thought, studiously tuned out in gym class, so much so that I had drawn the wrath of the taut, bristly haired neo-Nazi gym teacher, who accused me of being a slacker, a druggie, or both. I received a lot of detention that year and many laps around the gym, but I'd always kept my head down—or so I'd thought.

Despite the absolute terror of that moment, I experienced a quick moment of elation. Finally—I had *words*. These women knew what to call me, were able to name what I was. The elation rapidly reverted to fear. Others in the locker room that day watched what was going on. The gym-rat teacher was just around the corner in the alcove that shielded the locker room from the hallway. Certainly she heard the sound of my head hitting the locker. But no one turned around, much less came to my aid.

There was another problem. When the blonde she-devil breathed hateful words into my ear and painfully twisted my arm, she also—whether on purpose or not—pressed one firm, round hip against me. The fear and pain was quickly followed by desire. I despised her yet wanted nothing more than to get on my knees and plead for my life—and then kiss her, lip to lip.

In hindsight, I realize those girls didn't catch me in any overt illicit act; instead they slyly intuited my difference by noticing not what I did, but what I didn't do. These were belles—perfectly schooled in the soft, seductive drawl, the "oh, shucks" tilting inward of the knee, the gaze of rapt, mindless adoration—and they were tuned precisely to the boy channel. I, on the other hand, didn't talk about boys, or think about them, or pay them any particular attention, except perhaps to shuffle around them as they formed noisy packs in the halls. The girls in gym class noticed this, and their more comprehensive knowledge of the sexual world, along with their general predatory natures, helped them figure out the rest.

Later that week, I crept into a back corner of the library, hovered over the unabridged dictionary that lay open in the reference section, and looked up the words they had used to describe me. *Pervert* was disturbingly clear, *dyke* less so. *Lesbian* referenced the island of Lesbos, which I then found in the handbook to mythology. The island and its woman-oriented inhabitants were dismissed as "mythical," as in imaginary. Too bad there was nothing mythical about the skin sheared from my chin, the painful ache in my twisted shoulder, or the purple-blue bump on the bridge of my nose.

I often wonder what it would have been like if I had been able to go home, fall into my mother's arms, have her put ice on my bruises and take my side against this awful treatment—and then call the school principal, demanding that he put the screws to the Terrific Trio who, as the weeks went by, never missed a chance to smack me with a book or clip me from behind and into a wall or bank of lockers.

That didn't happen with my mother.

A LOT OF CHANGES had occurred between my first and my second coming out. My father had died and my mother remarried. We moved from northwest Florida to the outskirts of Atlanta, and I began high school (eighth grade in Georgia) in a vast brick complex that contained more people than the entire county where I had spent most of my life. If school was a vortex of confusion and pain, home was worse, the gym class bruises a mere variation on the ones that came my way at home.

In what became an all-too-predictable scenario, my mother's husband would finish his shift and arrive home smelling of malt liquor and in the frame of mind to find something not quite right with my sister and me. Sometimes it was because we left a glass in the sink. Or we walked into a room. Or blinked. Or breathed. In a mounting rage he would demand of my mother an explanation for why she had produced two such miserable creatures. Whether out of spite or fear—I'll never know—rather than protecting us, she usually wound up telling him to *take care of it*. Which he did.

As time passed I came to believe as the girls in my gym class did that I was a pervert. Apparently my mother believed it, too; that must have been why she didn't stop my stepfather. Maybe she thought that, as one of *those* people, I deserved whatever he dished out.

As for the assaults at school, of course I wasn't the only kid to be targeted. Any pudgy, blushing new kid was inevitably pinballed down the hall between laughing, well-muscled guys who teased, "Want me to call your mama, little boy?" The skinny, nerdy guys preempted torture from the jocks by picking one of their own, punching him in the arm, and snarling "faggot!" Most likely they all were straight, but their negative brain-brawn ratio ensured that they could never enter the pantheon of gods and goddesses that ruled every Southern high school: at the apex, the football jocks and cheerleaders, then basketball jocks (and cheerleaders), lesser athletes (all other sports), really rich kids, really good-looking kids, and really crazy/funny kids.

One poor guy was discovered in the boys' locker room wearing a training bra and girl's panties. He got roughed up and wandered around for weeks in a panic-punctuated daze. He was absent for a while. Then he reappeared, beatifically calm, in a frilly blouse, a pink sash in lieu of a belt, and caked-on blue eye makeup. The jocks were so stunned at his audacity that they didn't even go near him. Everywhere he walked, a wide, quiet space would open up in front of him then gradually close behind.

One day a guidance counselor crept into study hall and guided him carefully out and down the hallway. The next week he was absent. The week after that, a rumor tore through the homerooms that he'd tried to kill himself. I had no real sympathy for him. Why call attention to yourself? Why beg for it? The only way to survive being different was to be invisible or find a way to blend in.

For me, temporary salvation was of the blending variety, in the form of a short guy with transparent-blond hair, a toothy grin loaded with braces, and a twitchy, off-beat sense of humor. We didn't need more than a couple of careful, coded exchanges to realize we were in the same boat. And so we did what any two gay kids trying to survive would do—we went steady. And we thereby stepped into a separate universe. Sure, other kids still laughed at us. But, they did so because we were a very odd-looking couple, not because we were a couple of queers. The Trio occasionally growled in my direction, but they kept their hands off. It was a small breath of life.

A MORE PERMANENT SALVATION came at age sixteen. I bailed out of my mother's house and lived with a family across town until I finished high school. No one in this home hit me, and I navigated the rest of high school underground but untouched. A few days after finishing high school I moved from Georgia back to Florida to live with my paternal grandparents, and I vibrated around the edges of the safe, strong net they and my aunts, uncles, and cousins created.

In the meantime, I worked hard to convince myself that I was better off being asexual. I slept with a couple of guys. Felt nothing. Watched a guy fall in love with me. Felt guilty. Fell in love with a zany earth-mother type who wrote me poetry and held me to her ample, braless breasts. She backhanded me when I kissed her. As I picked myself up off her polished pine floor, I vowed that was the last time I would ever allow myself to feel. Period. I went to a few sleazy women's bars. Developed hopeless crushes on a few married women. Mostly I kept to myself.

Then I moved back to Georgia. A community college teacher convinced me to apply to Agnes Scott College—named after the founder's mother—and to my amazement I was accepted. It was a postcard-perfect Southern college: stately oaks shading neat brick buildings with wraparound porches supported by tall, white columns. Varnished wooden benches invited from the shade of massive magnolias, blossoms profuse enough to intoxicate with their scent. Carefully tended azaleas bloomed in every color—white, salmon, pink, red, variegated. In the summer, sidewalk edges were thick with daylilies.

Like many women's colleges in the 1970s and 1980s, however, the reality was not quite so pastoral. On the outside the college continued a pitched battle against the forces that decried single-sex institutions, especially female ones. It feared becoming a footnote in the history of women's education or—worse—an example of the wrongheadedness of such a vision.

On the inside, the school was steeling itself against the lavender magnolia menace. Students were cautioned against it. Deans were on the lookout for it. Gay teachers (there were a few) moved quietly to the deepest recesses of the closet. The straight women morphed into khaki-skirt-clad stereotypes of uber-femininity. The other three of us skulked around and eventually found one another.

BY THEN I HAD had two coming out experiences—one

inadvertent, one brutal. In both cases, fear drove me back *in* as soon as I could figure out how to get there. As I watched the world around me, I sometimes daydreamed how life would be if one day I awakened and found myself blissfully paired, traveling the same road as all those other he's and she's.

Despite the less than congenial surroundings, when I was twenty I finally came out to myself. Through a series of unlikely events, I wound up in the lap of a vastly nearsighted, incredibly luscious-chested woman. We kissed until our lips were raw. And each time I returned to her mouth, felt my tongue twine and unravel with hers, each time I let her hand find and stroke me, I knew with a clarity beyond denying that this was what I was about. Six months later, she abruptly decided she was not gay and went off in search of a boyfriend. When she told me, I mumbled something about maybe I should go and do the same thing. She looked me in the eye, said, "Oh, no, sweetie. Absolutely not. You totally dig women."

And it's true. I totally dug some lovely women. And finally, oh finally, I settled down with one. Because life seldom has any ironic deficiency, she had been married, had kids, and never did (and still does not) define herself as gay. At this point, however, semantics don't much matter. What is important is that nearly twenty years ago she fell in love with me, and vice versa, and I am the best and only woman in her life.

And oh, yes, I moved north—waaaaaay north—to her home in Connecticut.

We had been living together for more than a year when our phone rang. It was my nearly ninety-year-old paternal grandmother who asked, "So, when am I going to meet this woman you're living with?"

I said, "Um . . ."

"I think so, too. Christmas is good. See you then."

My partner noticed that I was standing, phone in hand, my mouth working like a beached fish. When I managed to speak, I said, "We've been summoned."

My grandmother had decided to put an end to the tacit agreement—on both sides of the family—that whatever we were, or did, or felt was not to be discussed.

My partner gently asked: "Does your grandmother realize that we have to drive almost thirteen hundred miles to see her?"

"I don't think she cares."

A few days before Christmas we packed. We drove. We negotiated our collective anxiety, the miserable traffic, and an ice storm which we periodically wished would sweep us off the road and into a ditch.

I knew my grandmother loved me. She claimed often that she had no problems "whatsoever" with God, only with God's people, whom she perceived as a hypocritical, backbiting pack of judgment and misery. When I lived with her, she had never pushed me to date guys and had quietly deflected any well-meaning folks who tried to "move me along." But I was also conditioned to a world that didn't much care for people like me. Maybe my luck had run out with her, too. I was pretty sure she'd like my partner as a person, but I wasn't sure what she'd do about the *partner* part. And the thought of being turned out of her world was unthinkable.

As we drove, the ice storm of Virginia gave way to chilly fog in North Carolina and Georgia, and finally we entered the pale December warmth of north Florida, the pecan trees bare, clumps of mistletoe decorating the branches. We got out of the car, stretched, and had a glass of iced tea.

After our greetings my grandmother didn't waste any time. She instructed me to unpack the car, get settled, and "stay inside." To my partner she said, "Let's just take us a walk."

They were gone for an hour and a half. When they came back, my partner made a beeline for the restroom, with a quick grimace as she dashed by. My grandmother approached and studied me for a long moment, then put her arms around me and nestled her head under my chin. I didn't breathe.

"She's a keeper," my grandmother said. She stood back, took my hands, and told me how she'd always worried about me. That I was never quite the same as the others. That she'd wanted to help but she didn't know how.

"She's the one you've been waiting for, isn't she?" It was a statement as much as a question.

"She's the one."

"Well, that's that," she said, linking her arm through that of my partner who had emerged from the bathroom. "I'll never have to worry about you again."

Soon after we returned from our visit, the phone calls began from the aunts and uncles, "just saying hello" and inviting both of us—always both—to visit, to call, "y'all don't be strangers," even though we lived far away. We lingered over the phone calls, played the messages on the answering machine over and over.

"Granny's been a busy girl," my partner said.

"Yes, she has," I agreed, adding: "You're in. And we are definitely out."

6.

Mississippi Middle School

Lessons on Gender and Class

⇒ JACK ⇐

FIRST GRADE

I wanted the watch with the compass for my birthday, but because that one was a boy watch, I got one with stupid Mickey Mouse hands instead.

"Now isn't that fun?" Mamma asked, but all I could think of was how was I going to navigate in the woods when we were playing spy if I didn't have a compass?

THIRD GRADE

I was put in the gifted class. We left our regular classes every Monday and Wednesday afternoon to learn about special things like space shuttles and computers. Everybody in the class was white, and I was the only girl. My best friend Anna wanted to be in the gifted class, too, but she didn't pass the tests.

Our teacher was Mrs. Martha, and she let us out fifteen minutes before all the other kids got to come out for short recess. In first and second grade, I had played with Kecedrick and Dedrick, who were black, and Anna, who was white, every recess. Now I played only with the white boys in class and we always played X-Men. They made me be Mystique because I was a girl and because they needed a bad guy, but I got to be Wolverine sometimes. He's the strongest, and his suit is yellow, which was my favorite color. My mamma was always mad at me because I played with the boys and avoided Anna and the other girls at recess. But all the girls just stood around talking and it was boring.

One time when I wanted to be Wolverine, Ryan told me I had to be Mystique and I said, "No," but he said, "You can't play unless you are."

"I can play if I want, and you can't stop me," I shot back. He raised his fist as if to hit me, so I hit him first in the stomach. He punched me in the mouth. I swung again, but it didn't matter. He simply grunted, whereas I was lying on the ground with a bloody nose and lip. As he walked away, I yelled after him: "Where're you going, chicken? We're not done!" He didn't even turn around.

JACK is a white, queer, able-bodied, gender-queer who lives in New York. Jack uses the pronouns ze, zir, and zirs in place of s/he, him/her, his/hers, respectively. Ze grew up middle and upper class. Jack left Mississippi at fourteen  and gets back far too rarely to see zir family. Since this essay was written six years ago, Jack has come out to zir grandmother and extended family who threw a barbeque and hugged zir partner. Zir parents visit NYC to see zir and zir partner every year. Jack does community organizing work.

We rode the church bus to choir every Tuesday afternoon. My parents had been going to the First Baptist church since we moved to town when I was three. Many of the FBC families had lived in town for generations. They lived in the country club neighborhood and owned stores and companies in town. Only white kids went to First Baptist then, and they were mostly the popular ones. We had snacks and playtime before we went in to choir practice. The boys played tag football, and the girls sat on the picnic tables and the jungle gym watching. I wanted to play, but they wouldn't let me. "Girls can't play football," Will Lee sneered at me. I could jump off the top of the jungle gym though, and not even all the boys would do that because they were scared. James sat on the jungle gym with me most of the time. He wouldn't jump and he didn't play football, either. I thought James was dumb. The other boys picked on him.

After recess at school one day, I stood behind James in line at the water fountains outside the girls' bathroom. As he turned to walk back to his class I shoved him. "Stupid!" I cried. He threatened to tell my mamma, so I said I was sorry.

Third graders got a longer recess on Tuesdays and Thursdays. Once at long recess, all the boys from church were playing football. When I tried to play, too, Will laughed and said, "All the teams are already picked; there's no room," even though the teams were uneven. I picked up the football tee and chased him down and hit him with it. He told on me after recess and Mrs. Louis, our teacher, asked me if "young ladies" hit people. I wanted to tell her that if they knew Will, they would. Instead I just shook my head, but I still had to stay in for the next recess. I felt really ashamed, but I didn't understand why. I thought Will deserved to be hit.

FOURTH GRADE

My cousin Zach is only one week older than me but he got to start deer hunting while I had to wait another year. I knew it was because I was a girl even though my daddy said it wasn't. I was so mad at Zach. He showed me all the cool Ninja Turtles he had gotten at his birthday party. I got stupid Barbies. I hated being a girl. Girls always got useless toys.

FIFTH GRADE

I gave up on playing football during recess. I was embarrassed at not being able to make the ball spiral like the guys, and besides girls weren't supposed to play. I stood talking with a group of girls like I was supposed to. It wasn't always that simple. There were four clusters of girls. Girls from different groups might talk to one another, but their little clumps were in pretty much the same spaces on the playground everyday. There were the black girls. They all stood together. Some of them played basketball with the boys occasionally. Then there were the "white trash" girls. They were the ones expected to get pregnant before they graduated. I think all of them had older siblings who caused trouble, or at least that's what I heard a teacher say about one of them. Then there were the popular white girls. They flirted with the popular white boys. Will Lee was the most popular, and he was dating Lindsey Allen, the most popular white girl. My friends and I weren't popular. There were only four of us, and somehow we didn't fit either of the other white girl groups. We didn't have quite the right . . . something. But we weren't considered trash, either; we did too well in school and didn't live in the trailer parks. In my case, I went to the "right" church and my family was probably the wealthiest of our foursome.

We liked to make fun of Will and Lindsey because they'd

already decided what they were going to name their dogs when they grew up and got married. Slick and Cool are stupid names for dogs.

We'd talk with Chris and Eric at recess. When Eric would say he couldn't hit girls, sometimes I'd hit him because he wouldn't hit back. What difference did it make that I was a girl? If he was stupid enough not to hit me back because I was a girl, he deserved to get hit.

SIXTH GRADE

I was at my uncle's house. Zach and I were supposed to go deer hunting, but I had just gotten my period for the first time—another reason being a girl sucked. I shoved as much toilet paper as possible up my vagina and went hunting anyway.

It was Wednesday night, and we were on our way to church for dinner. Mamma looked over at me. "You look like a boy," she said, "with that sweater and the jeans and those shoes. Can't you wear something that looks girlish?" She paused and added, "And you lumber along like a football player. Walk more gracefully." I looked at my father for some support, and he shrugged. "Your daddy thinks so, too," she finished.

We were sitting in Sunday school. The class was divided into fifth and sixth graders and girls and boys, and we sat at separate tables. I had been trying for weeks to learn how to doodle. It was what the other girls did while they listened to Miss Claire, our Sunday school teacher. I didn't know how. Maybe if I did, I'd fit in better. I'd been watching them and trying in the margins of my Sunday school book. I practiced writing my name in bubble letters, but it never looked quite right. It was like everything else. My clothes, my hair, my body—I couldn't figure out how to be like the other girls. All my clothes came from secondhand stores because Mamma believed in careful shopping. She taught me to look for well-cut designs and quality fabrics, and I found clothes I never could have afforded otherwise. Still, I was wrong somehow. Maybe it was because I was too fat. When somebody's mother told me, "Your calves are large . . . and strong," one night at a softball game, I knew she really meant *gargantuan*. I studied Lindsey Allen's body trying to figure out what it was about it that was attractive and how mine differed, but I worried that looking at her ass made me gay. I concluded I was a failure as a girl.

Because James and I went to choir, Bible Drill, Girls in Action, hand bells, and Wednesday night dinner with all the popular kids at church, I got invited to all their parties. So did James. I'd walk with him some afternoons when we went from school to church. I didn't talk to him in school, though, except to make fun of him, and the other church kids didn't really talk to me. We had unspoken rules.

Sixth graders of a certain race and class had dance parties for their birthdays. Parents would clear out the garage or rent a space and fill it with food and set up a stereo. Then they'd disappear into the house or woodwork. It was Dave's twelfth birthday party, and we were all gathered inside his parents' garage. On one side of the garage, I was talking with girls I kind of knew from church. The guys were all standing beside the food table on the other side, and Will and some other guys were needling James about something. He walked over and asked me to dance while they laughed. I realized suddenly that was what they were teasing him about. I told him, "No," but as he walked away I went after him, and when he turned around, I punched him. He stepped back, shocked, and I went to punch him again. I missed, and he ran. I ran after him, grabbing him and pushing him down to the grass. I heard a boy yell, "Jesus, James, can't you even fight a girl?" I sat on top of his chest while he squirmed, trying to get away, to move his arms, to shield his face. I punched him in the chest, on the face, on his side, while Will and a few boys stood around us. One of them hollered, "Hit him harder!" Another yelled, "Don't let him up!"

James quit squirming, and I suddenly realized what I was doing. I climbed off him and turned to walk away. Walking back to the garage, I was unsure of what to do. I didn't know why I had beaten him up, and I didn't know how to act afterwards. I felt horrible about what I had just done and totally confused. I walked over to the boys from X-Men and those gifted class days, leaving the girls and moving away from Will and Dave. I was standing there awkwardly when Dave's mother came out and asked me to come in the house. I expected her to be angry and yell at me, or to call my parents and make me leave, but she seemed confused as well. She told me not to hit James again and sent me back outside as if nothing had happened. I tried to pretend nothing had and so did everyone else. When another kid said that James had left and was walking home, Dave's mother sent her husband after him in his truck. James lived all the way on the other side of town—nowhere near Dave's house.

The following Sunday, as I walked into the church sanctuary, somebody's father stopped me. "I hear you beat up James," he said, raising one eyebrow disapprovingly. He was the only adult to ever mention the incident after the party, but the kids were a different story. James got teased endlessly for getting beat up by a girl. "Pussy boy," "Wimp," "Faggot," they called him. I left him alone. What do you say after you're that mean to someone? I tried to forget about it and threw myself into make-up and hair-do efforts, leaving the house with an obvious L'Oreal base line along my jaw every day and clippies acquired from Claire's at the mall holding my hair in place. I tried harder with the clothes, too, buying a pants suit like the one I saw a popular heavier teenager wearing at a state 4-H conference. I prayed for a good sense of humor; I figured being funny was going to be my only path to friends. And I helped Will and his friends cheat in pre-algebra when they asked, hoping that then they would leave me alone.

HIGH SCHOOL AND COLLEGE

I spent years trying to forget my childhood in Mississippi and did so pretty successfully. I had left for boarding school when I was fourteen and restyled myself in a place where class, race, and gender markings were very different, though no less influential. It was an extraordinarily wealthy and, to a lesser degree, white institution, and so were most of the students. My grandfather had died, so suddenly we could afford the tuition. I was amazed by the way I saw folks spending money. We all had the same uniforms in and out of class, ate in the same cafeteria, and lived in the same dorms. But only the rich kids were in the equestrian programs or played hockey, and only certain kids got to go on the mission trips at spring break. I knew my parents couldn't afford any of that even though we could afford to pay full tuition. My class status in Mississippi had been a largely ambiguous position. I moved in the white old-money social circles of my peers at church and just outside that circle at school, the boundaries maintained less by my actual class status than by my myriad of social failures. In high school, I found myself similarly positioned socially, though for slightly different reasons. Class status was not a remarked-upon topic, unless we were discussing the largesse of some of our incredibly wealthy peers.

In middle school, my friends and I hadn't fit into the popular crowd because of class status, but more importantly because we weren't shaped quite right (too fat and too thin), because we were too smart, and because we wore the wrong clothes (too masculine, too modest, too old and out of style). But at boarding school, there had been enough misfits to constitute our own group, and such differences were no longer a social death knell. There was a whole group of nerdy kids, mostly girls, primarily local and attending as staff or faculty children, or on scholarship. Being a girl in that circle didn't center on getting a boyfriend or being Barbie-esque, and my failings were no longer as debilitating. That didn't make boarding school an ideal place, however. Class, race, ethnicity, and nationality were never discussed in any real sense; treatment of such issues was relegated to a superficial celebration of multiculturalism. And misogyny, which was rampant on the social scene, was tacitly supported by the institution.

I had made a space for myself as a clown, cultivating an eccentric image on campus, and joined various organizations that celebrated the cultural components of racial and ethnic identities, without ever considering my white privilege. My group of friends was much more racially and ethnically diverse than the one I had left behind in Mississippi. Racial segregation was not a central organizing factor as it had been in my childhood. Still the institutional silences around inequalities impacted our conversations. Though we talked about ethnic or individual experiences and concerns, we never connected them to broader social systems of racism and classism. Like most of my friends, I escaped the worst effects of misogyny by avoiding the dating scene entirely.

In college I would find more freedom and a wider range of possibilities and remake myself again, coming out as queer and then as trans and gender-queer. I learned about power and privilege and social identities, and I found myself thinking back to grade school, to that time I had beat up James, and reflecting on how I had gotten to that moment.

In sixth grade, I couldn't have explained why I attacked James. I didn't have the language for so many things in my life. The interpretive and analytical tools I gained after middle school have helped me sort out my role as a child and since in perpetuating not only James's oppression, but also larger systems. James was a scapegoat—an easy target. Working-class and gender-atypical for our small Mississippi town, he didn't have the social capital to launch an effective response when I picked on him. I had known that at some deep level.

I had made fun of him like people had made fun of me—neither of us fit. None of my responses to the impositions of gender limitations worked. Being a girl proved crappy, and I was crappy at being a girl. But I couldn't be a boy, either, no matter how much I prayed. It wasn't just sports or being unable to write with the feminine curves of the bubble letters. It was everything I wanted to do. I was trapped by a rigid system that enforced gender binaries, and I took my frustration out on James.

I am responsible for what I did to him, but I was also middle-school society's blunt instrument gone awry. My abuse of James kept him in his place, replicating larger social oppressions, but the physical violence I enacted threw our microcosm out of balance. What I did was wrong—not just morally, that was obvious, but also socially. I was a girl; I wasn't supposed to beat anybody up. I tried to out-boy the boys, only to realize that no performance of masculinity, no matter how "good," would win the social approval or legitimacy I sought. James's request to dance was yet another unwanted marker of a gender I felt little affinity with, and the impetus for that request was a reminder of exactly how similar the two of us were. No matter how much I desired to put myself above him in social rankings, our peers saw us as linked by the nature of our shifting class and gender failings.

We weren't the same, though, and the fact that I never got in trouble was one illustration of our differences. James lived in the poorer part of town, and his mom didn't socialize with anyone who could have told her what I or other kids did to him. Or maybe they did, and she felt unable to respond. Stereotypical gender expectations played their part here, too. Though we both were ostracized for failing to adequately perform our prescribed genders, James was given significantly more grief than I was. I can only guess at how confiding to someone in authority might have reinforced his humiliation. To get any effective redress, he would have had to publicly confess that I beat him up—an acknowledgment of his "failure" of masculinity. On my part, that I was a white middle-class girl made my actions incomprehensible. While "white trash" boys and girls and boys and girls of color could get in trouble for fighting, the mirage of the Southern Belle, a good Christian girl, must have hovered over me. People couldn't reconcile that with the reality, so they let the reality go.

INTO MY TWENTIES

It's been more than ten years since I've been back to Mississippi for any extended period of time. I'm no longer a girl. I am constructing a more ambiguous body and my gender expression combines femininity and masculinity in some third space beyond man or woman. Still, when I do happen to encounter church folks or my parents' acquaintances in the grocery store, the girl archetype is still very much in play. Southern politeness, combined with an insistence on ignoring queer difference, leads them to awkwardly ask questions about when I'm getting married or if I have any kids yet, despite my testosterone-induced masculine appearance. My parents would prefer that I avoid public appearances altogether when I'm in town. My visible queerness is too confusing. They don't understand why I want to look like a boy and yet wear a dress occasionally, why I love my vagina and yet cut off my boobs, or why I use pronouns they've never heard before. They see these things as contradictions, as fantastic disregard for what they perceive as the reality of men and women, and only men and women. As strict Southern Baptists they struggle between their conviction that I am morally wrong and their love for me, their only child. I think my mamma is pretty sure I am going to hell, though she has never said so. She tells me she thinks I am drifting away from God and that she prays for me. I try to think of how to tell her I don't believe in *her* God, or, for that matter *any* God who condemns folks, and I worry that it will break her heart.

Last year my parents came to visit for Christmas. They drove twenty-four hours and spent less than forty-eight hours in town. I can't imagine anybody loving me more than they do, yet I know almost no one who understands me less. I talk to them every Sunday, but our conversations are a careful balancing act. We walk a fine line between the week's stories to which they can relate—and by listening, tacitly accept me—and those conversational roadblocks that would require them to acknowledge things about me that they are not yet ready to do. Mamma refuses to call me Jack, preferring instead to revive every childhood pet name she ever uttered. She calls me Prissypot, trying to re-feminize me and return us to a "pre-queer" time. She refers to me as her daughter instead of her child. But she also picks out ties for me when we go shopping at my favorite second-hand stores and fingers suits so she can tell me about their fabric content and quality.

Daddy tells me about the farm, about hunting when it's deer season, and asks about my car and the weather. He doesn't ask about my job since I work with queer students, and he doesn't ask whom I'm dating or how it's going. He's brought up my being queer only once since I came out to them. We were talking about how Mamma was dealing with it, and he said, "I try to avoid talking about it as much as possible."

When I drove to Mississippi two summers ago to introduce them to my girlfriend, they did not know what to do. Daddy met us down at the farm where we spoke for a few minutes about how my car was doing and about the nature of pickup trucks. He shook her hand, hugged me, and got back on his tractor and continued bush-hogging. Mamma refused to come out of the house as we sat in the car in the driveway. For her, I think meeting my girlfriend was tantamount to acknowledging my sexuality. Although I think they have suspected my queer identity since I was little, interpreting my desire for "masculine" things and styles as harbingers of gayness, openly acknowledging it is too difficult. They expended tremendous energy policing my behaviors and attempting to "save" me, but I'm not sure they ever articulated exactly what it was they were attempting to save me *from*.

I doubt gender-queer possibilities ever occurred to them. They don't fit with their Southern Baptist morals or their conservative gender conceptions. My parents are products of a dominant American, and a particularly Southern, culture that refuses to acknowledge any number of things. Like many Americans, they don't acknowledge the racism that divides the community and prevents folks of color from feeling comfortable in their church. They don't acknowledge the intersection of sexism and racism that stereotypes black girls as better athletes on the playground, but privileges white girls on the basketball team. They don't acknowledge the classism that operated on either side of me—locking me out of some social circles, while allowing me to escape to a better education at boarding school. I let most of that stuff go. Sure, I point out inequalities and assumptions, but I rarely think about returning to Mississippi to do that work in any real sort of way. I've followed injustices elsewhere, organizing in other communities and making them my home. The geographical distance has afforded me opportunities to live outside the insular white spaces of my childhood and parents, to learn in spaces where empowerment and liberation are goals, where feminist and anti-racist principles are primary tenets. But, it also has meant a separation from my past that I never intended. Each new self-formulation has moved me further away from that sixth-grade self in good and bad ways. Embarrassed by that person, I have set her aside. But recently I've begun to wonder what it would require of me to take on that old self, to make Mississippi feel safe for the different versions of me, and to incorporate her more fully into my understanding of who I am now. I wonder what it would require to break those oppressive silences. The same silence that kept me out of trouble for hurting James when I was in middle school discourages discussion of my operation or the effects of social identities, not just on individuals, but on the larger communities within which we live. It is a silence that makes us all less whole.

We seem to think that by ignoring oppression we avoid it. This rings true especially for children who are often imagined as innocent and free of all society's evils. But children operate and learn within our oppressive systems, and the dynamics around those identities we never explicitly talk about in school play out in much the same ways they do in the adult world.

I knew the rules of oppression long before I learned the language. I knew how to play on my white privilege to get out of trouble even before I knew what racism was. I knew to pick on James, a working-class white boy without the social capital to respond effectively. I knew that I didn't fit what a girl was supposed to be and that I couldn't be a boy. It is difficult to sort out the threads of power, privilege, and childhood reasoning that led to the pummeling I gave James, but it is necessary if I am to understand how I came to my current understanding and position within the world's webs of power.

7.

The Answers

⇒ CHRISTINA HOLZHAUSER ⇐

N elly Bechdel wanted me for Jesus when I was twelve. Mom pulled the car into the driveway of a brown trailer to introduce me to our new Bible school director, and I was surprised to learn that she lived so close to our town and that her dog was the one always running in the road when we came around the sharp corner. Nelly was tall and pale with thin gray streaks in her black hair, which was pulled into a ponytail at the base of her neck. Her mouth puckered like a cat's ass. She had narrow green eyes that bounced around while she talked, as if everything she had to say was written on tiny cue cards posted around the room: ceiling fan, glass coffee table, yellow shag carpet. I shook her hand. Though I was a little frightened, I told her I had recently started thinking about being a reverend. Her green eyes widened, "Has God called you?" she said, her head nodding yes.

In Sunday school I was the kid who could pronounce the words and interpret most of the stories. I loved words. Because I remembered the parables and discussed them with adults, they figured I was really interested and treated me accordingly. If that was what it meant to be called, then, by God, I was. I nodded my head. Nelly smiled. Her eyes were hypnotizing.

My hometown is tucked away in the Missouri River Valley. To leave it, you have to drive up a hill no matter which way you go. I've always loved driving up the steepest one because, if you really gun the motor, it feels like you just might keep going, soaring into the sky. But then, when you get to the top, there's the river down below and rolling hills for miles. There are three churches, the post office, and the bar. Portland was given its name because boats and carriages and trains would stop to trade goods. The men driving the conveyances might buy a hooker and have a beer. In the mid-1800s, two thousand people lived there; now there are eighty-five. The bar, more than a century old, sits just a couple of hundred feet from the Baptist church, which is just a couple of hundred feet from my house.

The Episcopal church, where my family goes, sits on a hill right across the gravel drive from my grandparents' house; a three-minute walk from my house. Still, we always drove. The church was built in 1909, around the time of the last economic boom—that was when the hotel still stood, and the bank and the brothel. The church's front door was painted red on red on red; it was several inches thick and made of heavy wood.

In the winter, Reverend Hyde's voice was hard to hear over the furnace kicking on and off in the back. I could see my breath most of those mornings, but the smell of old wood and Bibles made it bearable. When I was small, I would sink my incisors into the back of the pew in front of me, where people put their hands to get up from prayer. Touching the tip of my tongue to the soft, splitting wood, it tasted salty, like dirt.

The church asked me to be an acolyte when I was ten; the other kids in town didn't get there on time. Arriving at least fifteen minutes early, I would go into the dark little hallway where the old chifforobe stood. Reverend Hyde pulled his black robe from an old wire hanger and shook from disease as he put it on, mussing his hair in the process. Pulling my own velvety red robe from its hanger, I would put it on the same way he did, my hands high above my head like I was praising the garment first. On special occasions he wore different assortments of scarves, all shiny and silky with crosses and flowers. I began to imagine the day when I would wear one, too, the tassels tickling the waistline of my black robe, me standing up in front of people, inspiring them.

Atop the altar sat a cross and to each side candelabras held three candles each. I had been taught that one lights the candles on the right side of the cross first, starting with the one closest to the cross. Every Sunday I had to yell at the other acolytes to light the candles correctly.

"He ascended into heaven, and sits at the *right* hand of God the Father Almighty." Did no one ever listen to the Apostles' Creed?

On the few occasions when I got to ring the heavy bell at the beginning of the church service, I had to use my whole body to pull the rope; it made me feel powerful. It had a white sock duct-taped to it, maybe so the rope would be easier to

CHRISTINA HOLZHAUSER grew up in Portland, Missouri, a town of eighty-five. At eighteen she sped away toward Houston, Texas, to earn a BS in anthropology, but more importantly to get out and see the world. Since then she's worked as a pee collector at a nuclear plant, a histology technician, an archaeologist, an expert hiking-boot fitter, and a ranch hand in northern California. While living in a cabin with no running water in Fairbanks, Alaska, she earned her MFA in nonfiction. Christina now lives with her son in Columbia, Missouri. Her parents visit weekly and love being grandparents.

Ralph Horne

see in the dark, but it looked like a horse penis wearing a sock.

I had just memorized the Lord's Prayer and was moving on to the Nicene Creed, reading from the red book we kept at home on my piano. I liked the ceremony, the repetition of each sermon, the strange words that came from Reverend Hyde's gray, quivering lips.

We took communion once a month and I mouthed the words with him, watching as his shaky hand placed the little disc that looked like plastic in my cupped hands: "The body of our Lord Jesus Christ, which was given for thee, preserve thy body and soul unto everlasting life. Take and eat this in remembrance that Christ died for thee, and feed on him in thy heart by faith with thanksgiving." He spoke it like an old song, his voice rising and falling.

EVERY SUMMER WE HAD Bible school at the Baptist church. Afterwards, my mom would meet me and walk me home. Most of the other kids raced each other to meet their parents over at the bar, its screen door wiggling in its frame like a loose tooth, *slam-slam-slamming* as scabby knees scraped the torn screen and dirty feet pounded the thin, beer-soaked carpet. Kids begged for a dollar to buy beef jerky, Pepsi served straight from its cold glass bottle, and twenty-five cent pool games. Moms and dads, all drunk from too much Stag, stumbled off the blood-red pleather bar stools at two o'clock in the afternoon.

I know this because my grandparents owned the store most of my childhood, and all the kids in town caught the Number 2 school bus there every morning at seven o'clock. The parents had decided the bar was the safest place for all the kids to wait. We played red rover in the street and hide-and-seek around the Baptist church and the bar. Sometimes we'd go down to the Missouri River, only a couple of hundred feet away, and watch the older kids swing out over the water on an old rope, hoping they'd fall and make a sound louder than the rocks we heaved in.

So the first day of Bible school that summer, I bragged that I'd already met the new lady in charge and that she adored me because I admitted to being called by God. I didn't know if I was supposed to be a nun or a reverend since women weren't usually preachers, but being married to Christ seemed like a foolproof plan for me. Anyway, unlike everyone else my age, I wasn't that interested in dating.

"What man could beat that?" Nelly Bechdel had said when we met, meaning Jesus. I had seen her husband—a thin strip of a man kicked back in his recliner, his mustache the size of a bathroom rug—and I wondered why she hadn't chosen Jesus instead.

I always had boyfriends, though, and if they were nice I'd let them kiss me on the cheek. Copying my older cousin and some friends, I bought posters of Bon Jovi with his lips all pouty and his shirtsleeves ripped off. Another poster I put on my ceiling above my bed, like a friend had done. It was a picture of a man's ass and him holding roses behind his back. The caption read "Buns and Roses."

The stories of the Bible were fascinating to me because they were old, with those archaic words that were vaguely familiar, like remembering the feeling of a dream, but not the details. But I believed in God because I'd never been offered an alternative. I said the Lord's Prayer every night after I masturbated, worrying that I might do it too much and get so used to it that no man could do it as good as me.

I liked Bible school because everyone did. There were games, punch and cookies, and crafts. The lot of us sat kicking our legs for the first hour of sermons and songs, anticipating the Kool-Aid and thirty minutes of grass stains we'd get rolling around on the hill outside. I liked the ritual, too. Every day there was a song and a procession of all of the kids, with two kids leading the way, one carrying the Christian and the other the American flag. Always a serious song first: "Onward Christian Soldiers," maybe. But the next song we all looked forward to: usually "The Lord said to Noah There's Gonna Be a Floody, Floody," or my favorite, "I'm in the Lord's Army." It gave me goose bumps every time thinking of myself straddling a horse, the smell of sweat and leather, slashing the enemy. And not in the Army, but the *Lord's* Army. But the day Nelly was in charge, after the serious first song, the piano droned on, and she began the lyrics to another somber song while we all looked at each other in confusion.

I sat beside Will, my third-grade boyfriend, who earned the title after I read "James and the Giant Peach" to him on the bus because he couldn't. On the other side of me was Ben, a boy who had always had a crush on me. He was a troublemaker. His last name was Skelton, but kids called him Skeleton, and for good reason: he was skinny and ghostly white. Ben wrote me love letters and drew crayon pictures of us holding hands. I showed these to every girl in school and laughed and laughed, not really caring what he'd drawn or that he liked me. Later I realized he was skinny because he was probably hungry.

After the somber songs and nothing to lighten the mood, Nelly began to lead us in prayer that first morning, which we were used to. But after several minutes I could hear others shuffling and whispering. Trying to be mature, I held still, but I was wondering why we were still praying. Nelly hadn't said Amen, and it seemed as if she never would. Opening my eye, just so, I looked up at the pulpit, and there in front of the large oil painting of Jesus was Nelly, walking back and forth across the plush red carpet, her hands waving in the air, "Come forward if you want to be saved! The Lord Jesus Christ commands your love!" Until this moment, I'd never known of Jesus commanding anything. The picture of him behind her seemed so peaceful; I'd always assumed that Jesus said please and thank you. Every picture I'd seen of him he had long wavy hair, well groomed in a clean robe, a demure smile on his thin pink lips. To me, he did his dishes as soon as he dirtied them, and burned candles around the house for ambience. Even when he was hanging on the cross, the blood dripping from his ribs, he was still all lean muscle with no hair on his body except his nicely trimmed beard. He wore sandals, how mean could he be? But this new Jesus Nelly was talking about; well, I assumed he walked around breathing fire and screaming.

*God*zilla Jesus.

"Come to Jesus! Escape the fires of hell, come forward! You can be saved this morning!" Nelly screamed. Her eyes were shut tight, her glasses sliding down her pointy nose; her hair was coming loose from its ponytail and the stray gray hairs looked electrified.

The kids sitting around me were shifting. I kept telling myself Mom was in the back room, and *she* would save me when it was all over. Nelly kept praying, saying she wouldn't stop until someone came forward. The oldest person in the room was thirteen; all of the moms and dads were busy getting the classrooms ready, making Kool-Aid and snacks in the basement. Ben, always the trickster, smiled his toothy skeleton smile and walked toward the picture of polite Jesus at the front of the church. The room inhaled. We were worried what she'd do to him. We held our breaths, wondering if God would hate Ben, set him on fire right in front of us for not being sincere. But most of all, we wondered would it all be over and could we eat our cookies? Nelly laid her palm on Ben's forehead (were we supposed to watch this part or keep praying?) and blessed him. Ben was our savior and he hadn't been struck by lightning. We said some hallelujahs, and we were done, our necks stiff. We'd been praying hard for an hour.

That afternoon, I waited until Mom and I were safely in the house before I asked, "Am I saved?" Mom's response was to try to explain that Nelly was probably used to "teaching" adults, she didn't know how to talk to us. It was the first time I'd ever been scared by my faith. I thought Jesus loved me, the song said so, and in his pictures his hands were always open as if he were trying to fly away, or give me a hug. But Nelly's hands waving around, her feet stomping on the blood-red carpet, her voice wavering—those were things I had never seen before. No one had ever told me that God hated me and would punish me in hell if I wasn't saved.

"But Mom, am I saved?"

I'd gone to church, said my prayers, been baptized before I could walk. Everything they had told me to do so far, I had done just as they said. But now I was worried and I nagged Mom until she eventually answered, "I'll find out."

All that week the kids tried to avoid Nelly outside of our two-hour class with her. The next day she told us the story of Adam and Eve, her white hands high in the air: "Do you know why God called a woman a woman?" We didn't know. "Because when God pulled that rib from Adam and saw Eve he said, 'Whoa Man!'" She laughed. We laughed, looking out the sides of our eyes to make sure everyone else was doing the same. Ben wanted to know if it hurt Adam when a rib was pulled from him. Nelly said no, but we weren't so sure.

At the end of Bible school that long week, Nelly found me alone in one of the classrooms. She walked toward me, much taller than I thought, and said, "I have something for you." For all I knew, she was going to shoot fire out of her fingertips and cackle, but instead she handed me a Bible. She hugged me, and I liked it: this woman commanding me to give her a hug, her eyes that never looked away from mine.

I went home and opened the cover to read, "All of the answers are inside." For some reason, her words seemed comfort enough.

THE NEXT SUMMER I turned thirteen and Lisa, a young missionary, came to town. To my delight, she instructed a Bible school class for the week, and I was her special helper. I passed out Bibles when she asked, raced to answer her questions correctly so I could see her eyes light up and her plump cheeks turn pink when she smiled. Wanting to impress her, show her I had what it took to be a woman of God, too, I read passages every night from the Bible Nelly had given me so I could talk about them with her in the morning.

When the week was over I worried I would never see her again, but she stayed around town, teaching those who wanted to come the next month to a Bible study at the community building, a building that was once a one-room schoolhouse built in 1903. From my yard, I could look up the hill to the community building and see Lisa waiting there for my friend Shauna and me to walk up. The early morning sun cast her curvaceous shadow across the hill, lighting up her dark hair, darkening her already olive skin. Every time she saw me, she would put her arm around me and pull me in. It made me nervous, touching someone who worked for God. I wanted to be her.

Since it was summer, we sat outside under the shade of a covered cement pavilion, finishing up just as the sun soaked the last bit of dew from the grass. For a break, Shauna and I would see who could go the highest on the old swing set with the wooden seats. We'd play on the teeter-totter, each time

letting our asses hit the hard dirt in an attempt to throw the
other from her seat high into the air. We'd laugh and sling in-
sults all the while and talk about baseball, how we'd go ride on
the four-wheeler when we were done there. Lisa would glance
up from flipping through her Bible, not amused at all by our
jokes or stories of how we got the huge scars on our knees; I
imagined she just wanted to talk more about God. Not only did
Shauna not like Lisa, but she didn't like the Bible study either.
She'd make fun of me for wanting to go, for wanting to spend
time with Lisa at all. I'd push her and we'd wrestle. We acted
like this at school, too, especially in the long hall where our
freshmen lockers were located. One day she found me alone
in the hall, my back against my locker and tears in my eyes.
She made a joke and elbowed me and then realized it wasn't
like that this time.

A distant cousin had passed away. I had sat at her funeral,
the stiff wooden pew making me slouch. After the holy man
said some things, the music started. It was "How Great Thou
Art," and Tami's voice was singing it. I sat, looking at nothing,
chewing the insides of my mouth. I bawled, the blubbering kind,
but tried to keep still, tried not to let my shoulders heave, tried
to calm myself by thinking that she was with God in heaven
and I was just being selfish. After all, she was my second cousin
and I really only saw her once a year. But she was always so full
of energy, talkative, funny. She played with me even though I
was ten years younger. There was something about her face, her
blue eyes, her thin, pointy nose that always held my attention.

I had been to funerals before, enough to know the whole
routine, enough to know when to say *ashes to ashes*. But Tami
was dead. I had breakdowns for about a week. Mom wanted
me to talk about my feelings, but I couldn't without crying
and I felt stupid since Tami and I weren't even close. I wrote

poems by the river until the wind dried my tears.

I talked to God, asking if Tami was okay. I prayed more than ever. I prayed that God would send me a sign—even if it scared me—so I would know she was in heaven. I worded my prayers carefully, having learned recently that saying things like, "I'll quit masturbating if you help me get an A in math" was inappropriate. You should never try to make a bargain with God. So, I just asked politely, "If you could send me a sign, that would be great." I lay awake for hours watching around my bedroom for something to happen, for the dinosaur skeletons to dance or my softball medals to clink together. Once, I felt something warm on my hand, like another person's hand. I smiled. The next night I had a dream that Tami sat down with me at the bar. I was eating a cheeseburger, the grease dripping down my hand, and I asked her how heaven was. She said it was good. I reached out to touch her but she disappeared. I woke that morning and her death never bothered me again. I guessed I had to be a nun after that. Being the bride of Christ was sounding better all the time. God had chosen me. I started attending a Saturday night Bible study with kids from high school. Trying to find meaning in those words was so stimulating, and so was sitting on the couch with all of my friends, their thighs lined up like different colored piano keys, touching mine.

The summer before my sophomore year I taught Bible school with my Mom. I grinned at the kids with Kool-Aid moustaches and helped them get their cookies. We made pencil holders for Fathers' Day out of old cans of corn, and the summer felt especially important because of what had happened with Tami earlier that year.

When Lisa left town I asked for her address and she gave it to me. I wrote once a week, telling her I missed her, missed talking to her about religion. I told her how I couldn't wait until the next time we saw each other. Twenty-two and engaged, she replied to a couple of letters, but quickly lost interest in corresponding with a thirteen-year-old. When the letters stopped coming, I stomped through the bushes, refusing to use the small bridge that crossed over the creek behind my house. Grabbing broken branches and old saplings, I threw them across the water, letting them sink into the mud on the other bank before I would acrobat my way across to the post office. A nervousness was forever fluttering in my chest and I kept hoping a letter would come from the missionary.

MY JUNIOR YEAR OF high school, I had begged my parents to let me go on a trip to Europe with a friend a year older than me. It was her graduation present, so I presented it to my parents that way—an early gift for my graduation. I had never been on a plane, but I wasn't scared. I had a feeling that I had to go; I had written in my journal that there was more to the world and I was ready to learn about myself.

So it was in Westminster Abbey that I turned to whoever was behind me ready to spout off everything I'd learned in World History that semester: "Do you know where Lady Jane is buried?" What I saw were piercing blue eyes, a pointy nose, and tousled blonde hair. "Is it here or the Tower of London?" I said, hinting that I knew who Lady Jane was and that I had some idea of where I was in the world. She smiled, looked down at the camera hanging from her neck, "Dunno."

An hour later I saw her on the bus and realized she was in my tour group for the next nine days. She seemed shy and about my age—seventeen or so—so I sat beside her on the tour bus, introducing myself and asking if she had a seatmate. She said she was there with her little brother and shrugged her shoulders. I smiled, trying not to let the disappointment show.

A day later, at Anne Hathaway's house, our tour guide asked us to split into two groups, on the right under eighteen, on the left eighteen and over. I stepped to my under-eighteen line, looking around for my new friend, Laci. Then, I saw her across the room.

"How old are you?" I shouted across the gap.

"Twenty-one," she smiled, as she shrugged and played with the strap of her camera.

For some reason I found myself staring at her reflection in the tour bus windows as we drove through England, the thatch-roof houses flickering by like an old film reel, her face there, looking at the world. I worried that she could see me looking. She had on a Walkman and was nodding her head with the beat, wrinkling her eyebrows in a way that suggested she was realizing something with every thump of the bass drum. Every chance I had, I talked to her. I wanted to make her laugh, and then worried that I might have said something to offend her. I followed her through the old churches, taking the same pictures she took. There was something about her, maybe the way she walked or hunched her shoulders; I knew we were meant to be friends.

It was the seventh day of our trip and we were in a small town in Scotland. I had crawled out onto the roof of our guesthouse and Laci crawled out behind me. We could see the green hills and distant mountains; a haze was settling over the town below us. Visually retracing our walk from earlier in the day, we could see every little street, the sheep we fed grass to along the journey. It was like we were looking down on a clichéd model town in the Scotland highlands. That evening we had played like small children behind the house, crawling on our elbows like soldiers, jumping up to shoot at each other, fingers cocked and ready to fire. We laughed at ourselves, but we didn't stop.

Laci said she would love to get lost in those hills. I asked if I could come with her. Just us, then, we'd said. We'd live there and hunt and write poetry. We'd fill our days with nothing but the important things in life. And there would be music.

We talked about religion on the rooftop. I was convinced at that moment God existed. He had given me the opportunity to go on this trip, to see the sunset we were watching together, to meet Laci. I had always believed things happen for a reason, and I wondered what lesson she would teach me. I told her I was Episcopalian and asked which denomination she was. She laughed and said, "I practice Schmidtism." I assumed it was some Texan form of Christianity, but then she explained that her last name was Schmidt.

As I looked into her blue eyes against the backdrop of the wet-green hills she talked of how bodies are just made of energy. "Matter can't be destroyed, it rearranges. When we die, the energy just goes other places."

Science.

"You don't believe in God, then?" I asked, while looking at my shoes, thinking our friendship might have blown up in front of my face. The God I believed in had a white beard and lived somewhere at the top of the universe, like a puppeteer.

"Yeah," she said, "I do. But God is energy. God is too complex for humans to comprehend, so people have to invent Jesus."

Completely exhausted from the experiences of the trip, from nights of sleeping fewer than four hours, staying up late with Laci, I admitted through slurred speech that I'd never thought of the world that way. And science was something I understood. I had watched countless relatives as they lay in their coffins and pictured them decomposing underground. I had always understood that they just rotted and fed the trees, and wouldn't there eventually be too many souls in heaven, crowding up the place? Laci put words to what I dared not.

A lump had been growing in my stomach for days, ever since I had watched Laci's reflection in the bus window. I had quit eating, couldn't think. At nights all that went through my head was her name; sometimes I pictured it spelled out, L-A-C-I. My thoughts wouldn't stop. Her name ran in front of my eyes like a flashing marquee: *lacilacilacilacilaci*. Then it looked unfamiliar and weird. So, I sat on the roof with her just inches from me, and we stared down onto the town, and I let myself consider, for the first time in my life, that what I had been taught wasn't exactly the *only* way. If I was wrong, there was no heaven and that meant there could be no hell.

THREE DAYS AFTER WE parted at the airport an envelope came in the mail with something the size of a wallet bulging inside. I ripped it open and found a mixtape of eighties' new wave peppered with country and old swing, alternative. I listened to it all day, hearing music I had been only slightly aware of until then. And the lyrics, the words. The Smiths sang, "No it's not like any other love, this one's different because it's ours / I'll probably never see you again." Morrissey also sang, "Sing your life / don't leave it all unsaid somewhere in the wasteland of your head." And the Cranberries were there, too, like lips pressed to my ear whispering, "I can't be with you / 'cause you're not here." I sat by the river and listened. I listened in my bedroom with the window opened, crickets and cicadas croaking. I crawled onto the roof of our house and listened to every word, her name *lacilacilacilaci* still scrolling through my head, a knot massaging my stomach, then my throat. I kept the letter in my pocket all day, pulling it out with every song to see if there was something I missed.

The letters kept coming, telling me more about Houston,

how many things we could do, how much she missed me, how much she wanted to share her city with me. I sent one every day, too, saying the same. At the end of each letter we wrote song lyrics, three or four little lines until we said what we needed to. Sometimes, we used the same quote for more than one letter. The lyrics became my mantra. She wrote: *I'd waltz across Texas with you.* Every night before bed I pulled out my Oxford sweatshirt, the one I let her borrow on our last night together in Scotland: it smelled like her perfume and shampoo. Music filled my head so full I couldn't push it out even for the Lord's Prayer. I had read her letters so often they were tattooed on my brain and my prayer became one word over and over and over. Every morning that summer, I would speed walk to the post office, taking the road. I didn't want to waste time with trying to forge my way across the creek.

About a month after returning home from Europe, I convinced Mom and Dad to let Laci visit. They asked, "What does a twenty-one-year-old *woman* want with you?"

The first two nights we sat up talking and fell asleep in the same bed. For some reason, I found myself in her bed again the third night, talking into the early morning. All day we scratched at chigger bites we got by sitting in the wrong patch of grass; it became a game to catch the other and swat her hand. She was scratching while she was telling me a story, and we were lying on the quilt on Mom and Dad's antique bed. I reached out for her hand, to bat it away: "Stop scratching," I said.

But I didn't let go.

I stared at what I'd done, her hand in mine, wondering if I could play it off if I let go now, or had it been too long? I saw our whole trip played out in half a second, a hot surge of images that blinded me to reality. Suddenly, she was my boyfriend; I mean, we were holding hands and walking over the great authors' graves in Westminster Abbey. We were young lovers standing on Hadrian's Wall. Laci and I were holding hands. She smiled at me. We didn't move or speak. Eventually, I propped myself up against the headboard. She put her head on my chest and grabbed for my hand again. I twirled her hair around my finger staring at her like I'd never met another human, my heart beating like it might burst, my palms sweating. An hour later we kissed. My world exploded behind my eyelids. I knew what my friends felt when they talked about love, about sex; I knew why they wanted to spend time with their boyfriends. For a brief moment, I imagined my parents' reaction, my friends', the church's. But her face wasn't scratching my lips and she didn't smell funny like my boyfriends. When the kiss was over, all I could say was, "Girls are so soft."

DURING THE TWO WEEKS that I was preparing how to tell Mom and Dad I was in love with a woman, they were rummaging through my bedroom, trying to prove me guilty. "What are these?" Mom's knuckles were white against the red paper Laci had written on. What she found the most disgusting was a letter where Laci had written, "I miss you and can't wait to hold you again." At the bottom were Fine Young Cannibal lyrics, "She drives me crazy / like no one else." Dad stood, red-faced behind Mom while she read these lines and screamed, "What does this mean?" I stared through them, tried to picture the undercurrents of the river, those reeds that grow along the banks that you can take apart, piece by piece, Laci's blue eyes, the way kissing her was like eating a ripe peach.

I sat on the couch from three in the afternoon 'til seven that night listening to them.

"You want her to eat you out?"

"God does not approve of this!"

"You've never even been with a man," Mom said, stretching out one vowel into three.

"You won't live in this house," Dad said.

I had no defense. It was so new to me. Of course, I figured God didn't like it. I had quit going to church, afraid that I would spontaneously combust if I walked through the door. I had considered my fate of burning for eternity, wondered if it was only painful for a little bit, then maybe one got used to it. I had also wondered why God would make me fall in love with someone who was so obviously perfect for me and then burn me in hell. It seemed counterproductive. And really fucking mean. And Schmidtism was becoming more real all of the time. I had always believed in science, in evolution. I loved dinosaurs, so what *did* Jesus have to do with any of it? I never saw dinosaurs mentioned in the Bible, but they existed, there was evidence. And here were my parents, the most supportive and understanding people in my life, yelling words at me I had never heard them say. I curled into a little ball and closed my eyes, repeating the last song I had heard on a mixtape: *why are you so far away she said / and won't you ever know that I'm in love with you / you're just like a dream / just like heaven.*

It was three weeks before my senior year of high school. The haze of summer was still enough to choke a person, the humidity thick and cloudy like stew. And just as hot. I was sitting in a chair in Jefferson City, waiting for the therapist, or psychologist, or whoever to call my name. I hadn't said more than three words to my parents since they found the letters. Sometimes they'd try to fight, but I just ran to my room and played my tapes. Mom and Dad sat in the lobby, Dad's thick, sunburned arms crossed over his large stomach. His head turned away, the muscle in his jaw moving like he was trying to grind nutshells. Mom stared at me. So I slouched more in my chair and stared at my green fingernails, my shoes, my life. Mom had recently accused me of smoking pot in my room. It was just incense, I told her. And it really was. She frowned more every time, mad she was wrong or mad that I was sober.

My name was called—a relief to get out of the room where Mom and Dad were—and I was directed to a small office. I looked at the woman who sat behind the desk, her thick black hair short and spiky. She smiled. I had never been to a therapist, or anything of the sort. I made fun of people who went. I was preparing myself for a fight when she asked what was troubling me. I started, "I play varsity sports, I have a lot of friends, I'm president of three organizations at school, and my grades are excellent." Then I thought for a moment, picturing Mom and Dad in the lobby, and how happy they would be now that they were going to *fix* me, as they had put it. I looked her in the eyes, "Oh, I just realized I might be a lesbian." She sat back in her chair and asked how I was handling it. I played with my shoelaces and thought. "Well," I said, "it's kind of weird, but I'm dealing with it." She smiled and nodded her head, saying that was just great. Then she said, "It's probably your parents who need to talk to me." She ushered me back out into the lobby, and then I heard her say, "Mr. and Mrs. Holzhauser?"

Two minutes later and my parents were throwing open the door of the woman's office, holding hands. Mom's grimace was even tighter than before and they walked past my chair before I could say anything and she grabbed my arm and yanked me up like I was some little kid screaming on the floor of the toy aisle. I stumbled and caught my balance as she was pulling me out of the lobby. I looked back to the therapist's office, and she was leaning against her door frame, one hand in her pants pocket, the other kneading her forehead. "Thanks," I said, hoping she could hear me, hoping Mom and Dad couldn't, but then, not really caring. She crossed her arms over her chest, sighed. She never blinked, but kept looking at me, a corner of her mouth pulled tight, like someone trying to smile when her mouth is dentist-numb.

Over the next weeks, I was taken to several therapists. When they were done talking to me, they would inevitably call Mom and Dad into their office. And then we would leave quickly, the drive home filled with silence. I would pretend to sleep in the back seat, but my dreams were of Houston, a huge city where Laci promised I could be myself, go to museums, eat greekindianfoodwhatever. Gay bars. Dance clubs. Freeways winding around each other, like snakes coiled and waiting.

Dr. Mike was different, though. I sat, legs spread wide, my dinosaur socks pulled to my knees. Green Carhartt shorts, black and white wing-tip Dr. Martens, green stripes in my hair, a dinosaur t-shirt. His mustache twitched as he looked me up and down: "You know, Christina, you're different from most girls your age." Over several sessions he tried to convince me that being a lesbian in this world was too hard. I kept pointing out that I wouldn't be living in his world, a small Catholic town in mid-Missouri; I'd be living in a city of millions and believe it or not asshole other gay people existed in the real world. Then he told me that I should feel bad for my parents. They had adopted me and had hopes and dreams for me and I had dashed all of them against the rocks of heterosexuality, or whatever. Marriage, kids, a good life; he said I could never have those things now. I stood up, after weeks of listening to this man, after weeks of answering him in a way that was so sarcastic, it almost wasn't, and said, "It's good my parents raised me to be free-thinking and independent because I'm aware enough to know I'm smarter than you." And I left.

I wasn't allowed to write or speak to Laci. Every time I

answered the phone, Mom would pick up the other line to see who it was. Late at night, I would hide in my closet to call her from my T-Rex phone. We'd talk for hours about my freedom. About me going to college in Houston. Once, Mom found me on the phone and picked up. "Is this Laci?" she asked, sounding like she was nauseous, "I don't ever want you to speak to my daughter again. Understand?" And Laci, in her quiet, Texan way of speaking said, "I'm sorry, but I can't do that." Mom ordered her off the phone and I shouted *"Bei Mir bist Du Schoen,"* before I hung up, quoting a song she'd given to me.

A few weekends that fall, Laci drove from Houston to see me. An eight hundred-mile drive, arriving at night. We scheduled meetings on the Katy Trail, an old railroad track that was becoming a state park only a hundred feet from my house. I'd sneak out, something I'd never even cared to do, right down the steps to the front door that we never used, and then run into total darkness. With the river to my left, animals rustling in the bushes along the bluffs to my right, I'd jog a mile until I saw a human form coming at me. It rained once, so we huddled together under a piece of the bluff overhanging the trail. Like we lived thousands of years ago. We were primitive. And we held each other like that all night. Sometimes talking, making plans of when to meet again, or I'd ask to hear more about Houston. Sometimes we sat and listened to the rain fall. Once we saw a meteor shower. And we sang: *the stars at night are big and bright, deep in the heart of Texas.* Then, she'd drive home. Thirteen hours through the Ozarks, grasslands of Oklahoma, and Texas, listening to the tapes I'd made for her. And I'd sneak back in the house at sunrise, dazed from no sleep, and from the sight of Laci. In six months I had seen her for only four days and always in secret and darkness. Once back in my room, I'd get to sleep twenty minutes before I had to work or Mom and

Dad got up. It wasn't sleep, really, just a half-conscious dream replaying everything that had just happened, my shirt wrapped around my face because it still smelled like her, like the woman who could take me away from the small town I'd grown too big for. My savior.

MY GRADUATING CLASS HAD sixty-five people, the biggest class the school had ever graduated. I had known the same kids since kindergarten, knew their parents, their siblings, their dogs. But now they looked at me like they had never seen me before. Or they didn't look at me. People thought I was doing drugs because I started dressing differently, dying my hair weekly, wearing a chain wallet. In the locker room I changed in the bathroom stall. I showered first and ran out before I could be accused.

One day I found the word *dyke* scratched into my gym locker. Becky had commissioned Lindsay to do it, a freshman told me.

One day I came to school and my friend, Kristin, said, "Tell me you didn't try to kiss Julia."

"Yuck. No."

"Well, she's telling everyone you did."

One day I asked a lunch table full of friends if they honestly thought I was going to burn in hell. They stared at me. Some told me to read Leviticus.

That night I opened up the Bible Nelly Bechdel had given me; the one I had read for hours and hours. The one I hadn't touched since I came home from Europe in a daze. I read Leviticus 20:13: "If a man also lie with mankind, as he lieth with a woman, both of them have committed an abomination: they shall surely be put to death; their blood *shall be* upon them." I saw a loophole. It seemed the Bible was only talking about gay men, not women. I can't say I was comforted, but I had a plan. If there was a heaven, and it seemed highly unlikely there was, when I got to the gates St. Peter might say, "Aren't you a homosexual?" And I might say yes and then open up my Bible and point, "I don't see anything here about women." And St. Peter would stumble over words, check his references, and then, defeated, he'd motion me through.

My eighteenth birthday was January of 1998, the date I had been looking forward to, knowing Mom and Dad had no legal control over me after that. When they asked what I wanted for my birthday I told them, "I want Laci to visit and I want you to be nice to her." Dad laughed a little. And Mom said no. And we fought like this for a week, me yelling and hiding in my room like the typical teenager I never pictured myself becoming, them yelling back. Until one day, when I guess they got tired and said *okay*. Within three weeks she would arrive.

I sat staring at her, glancing only occasionally at the road as we drove to Columbia, a college town an hour from my house. We had decided to go there because it was a city by my standards and I knew there was a gay bookstore there. We held hands walking around downtown. One woman made a noise of disgust when she saw us, so I pulled Laci closer and we laughed. We watched a sad, skinny guy strum his guitar on the patio of an Italian restaurant, we drank five-dollar coffees. I was preparing for Houston.

I had applied to the University of Missouri in Columbia; Mom and Dad were happy to pay for all of it. I was also offered softball scholarships to other universities around the state. But I had applied to the University of Houston without Mom and Dad knowing. I waited for my acceptance letter, then, when it came I told them I was moving far, far away. But, they refused to pay if I went there, telling me they wouldn't support my *lifestyle*. Knowing they were more practical than hateful, I did the math and proved I would save them quite a bit of money by going to Houston.

I was driving, Mom in the passenger seat, a fully loaded CD rack wedged in between us, the car packed full of thrift store clothes and obscure music. We hit the top of the hill, the sky bright blue and cloudless. The sun was coming up in front of us over the river, lighting up the valley that was home. In the rear-view mirror the tiny river town I had grown up in was vanishing and I was soaring into the unknown.

In Houston, Laci and I left Mom at the airport, tears staining her face. We drove away holding hands, music blaring, like we'd gotten away with something, and I looked out at the skyline, trying out the new word in my head: *skyline*. Five million people were out there somewhere, in the cars circling the freeways, in their houses making love, in churches, clubs, and restaurants. And there was only one person among them all who knew who I was. The city radiated a glorious energy that filled the car and lighted my body.

8.

Love and Death and Coming Out

⟹ B. Andrew Plant ⟸

In tawdry novels and trashy television miniseries—which are so often set in my native South—many characters are overcome by melodramatic epiphanies: "Because of what he did to me I'm going to become the best darn businesswoman ever and take over his multinational corporation"— *that* sort of sweeping realization.

In real life, I've found that life changes and realizations are more gradual. They evolve, rather than hitting us all at once. Or maybe it's just that we're mostly creatures who learn our lessons slowly. More, "Oh, I think I'm beginning to get it now," and less, "Eureka!"

That slower process is how I came to be comfortable with who I am. Not that I had ever been completely terrorized by the thought that I am gay. I am lucky in that regard. Far too many folks have allowed the small minds of others and the wrongheaded notions of our collective culture—particularly our religious institutions—to make them feel they were bad for being gay. Religious gay guilt seems to be especially indigenous south of the Mason-Dixon Line.

Somehow (karma? divine intervention? a kindly she-god?) I always knew I was different, *and* I had an innate sense that this was not necessarily bad, or at least that I was not inherently bad because of it. Not that I didn't suffer because of my differentness, even when I didn't know what that differentness was all about.

I was derided by my father because I was not more manly. I was less than adroit at sports. I didn't relate well to boys in the neighborhood and even less so at school, where they could be cliquish and downright mean. I was called faggot. My reaction was the same as that of many other little gay boys who didn't yet know they were gay: I became the class clown.

It's a good defense mechanism. Or at least it's natural and a bit more comfortable than being constantly terrorized. Even so, it only goes so far with the kids I thought I wanted to like me. And, while it entertained the girls I wanted to be friends with (or did I want to *be* them?), it also seemed to repel them in equal measure; they labeled me immature. Better that than queer, I guess I thought at the time.

My education certainly suffered. I went to a good school system but one that, like most, had no real idea of what to do with a sissy who was sort of a loner and who was definitely achieving below potential. It's still too rare when a kid tilting toward homosexuality is treated normally by educators. Rarer still that he might actually be protected by them.

Instead, both educators and my parents—my father mostly, as is often the case with young 'mos—took the approach that if I would just try to fit in, if I would just try to be less nelly, people would stop picking on me and I would have an easier life. Indubitably, that misses a key point that they should have known and that my young mind couldn't yet know: I didn't just act different, I didn't just feel different, I *was* different. At least when it came to my budding sexual orientation.

So here I was, having learned by trial-and-error that I needed to hide my differentness, when I began realizing just what that differentness was. By sixth grade or so it had dawned on me that

I liked boys the way I was supposed to like girls. I didn't quite know what to do with that information, but I knew instinctively that this was not something you shared with others. Thank goodness I was blessed with that one bit of "shut-up-ness," as my East Tennessee granny would say, because I otherwise did not get the shut-up gene (especially not from her)—my judgment usually failed at deciding what to and what not to tell.

So I wasn't just different and tormented for it, I knew what the difference was and was tormented that it was a secret I had to keep. Still, all was not lost. You see, through minor social and media glimpses, I had been assimilating that there was gay life out there. I was not alone—well, maybe for now, but not forever. I somehow knew—maybe it was early gaydar?—that if I could survive junior high and maybe high school and maybe college, I could someday commune with other folks like me.

B. ANDREW (DREW) PLANT is an award-winning, self-syndicated columnist; his articles and op-ed features appear in leading national and niche publications, addressing LGBTQ, health, and social justice issues. For five years Drew wrote a feature column for *Southern Voice* newspaper. He was editor at large for *A&U*, a monthly non-profit AIDS magazine, and interviewed and wrote cover features about Hillary Clinton, Dolly Parton, Coretta Scott King, Patti LaBelle, Liz Smith, two White House AIDS czars, and

Robin Henson

other luminaries. His "day job" is as a public relations strategist. Drew lives in a low-slung ranch house in Atlanta with his husband, a dog, a cat, and two compost bins.

Mind you, I did not know this had a label: Coming Out. I just knew that, if I could hold on, I could someday be me—whatever that was. This is easier said than done, because the time between the beginning of about seventh grade and the end of college is significant. And, as many a gay and non-gay kid can tell you, junior high is a mean and nasty place.

AS OFTEN HAPPENS WHEN you have a plan, there are bumps in the road. The main bump I encountered was of the most natural kind—human nature. It's simple enough, really: I now knew a bit more about my true self, and whether or not I wanted it to, the real me was bound to pop out.

Sometimes I was encouraged to be myself, like when a talented and compassionate junior high school art teacher befriended me. She gave me both focus—a new interest in art—and a place to express myself—again, art. Such scenarios are a mixed blessing. You show a little more of yourself and get strokes for it from friends and an encouraging teacher; on the other hand, you get hammered all the more by detractors. Often, those detractors are simply intimidated by seeing the authentic you, but I didn't understand that then.

Being intimidated by authenticity should have been at least a bit more familiar to me; you see, I knew this phenomenon from the other side. Like many a young gay kid, I frequently pushed back the hardest against those who were most like me—like the kid who joined our class midway through my eighth grade and was, gulp, openly gay. I liked him, but I made fun of him and definitely made no effort to befriend him. You know, if I'm kind to him, people might think I'm queer! Couldn't have that.

My script and my journey changed again in high school. Things had become comfortable enough—thanks to great freedoms like driving and busy parents and the androgyny of some early eighties pop stars—that I began admitting to being bi. I now know that's a common theme for young gay men, but I found it a pretty cool compromise back then. So I had to sleep with a few girls; that was okay since it meant I could bag a few guys along the way.

That approach got me through high school; literally, right to the end of high school. Yes, there were confrontations in the hallways and confrontations at home. In the latter, the overriding theme again was, "You're bringing this strife on yourself—just change and it will all be easier."

DURING THIS TIME MY parents also subjected me to something else I now know was common for gay youth: evaluations by our family priest and by a religion-based mental health counselor. No surprise. Both told us that my soul was in danger if I did not change. Apparently, God would punish me for being me. I don't know if I was smart enough—because my good sense rarely prevailed otherwise—or if I was just irreligious, but it did not scare me that I liked other boys and that God ostensibly did not like it.

By high school graduation I had a boyfriend and the threats from my parents—my father, really—were on the rise. They wouldn't support me if I lived this "lifestyle." They wouldn't send me to college. They would have me committed. And so on. None of this will come as any surprise to gays of my Generation X or before.

Instincts—both good and bad—again kicked in and I bolted. The day after graduation I moved out—waterbed and all. To add to the drama, I did this stealthily. Everyone was away for the day at my sister's college graduation. She still hasn't forgiven me, but I did what I had to do. I had to be me, at least in some form or fashion, and at the time this seemed like the way.

That began a series of ill-fated college relationships, including a "starter marriage" to my first long-term same-sex partner that lasted most of the way through college. I worked nearly full time in college—as I had my last year of high school—so I didn't have to worry about letting the personal me out as often as I might have otherwise. I was at work when others were at frat parties.

That is a good message to young gays: Make financial independence a reality for yourself. I digress in saying this, but I believe it's a fundamental point those who are disenfranchised should learn early. In our culture, you can literally buy your freedom in some ways. You don't have to be a blinging high roller, but if you can pay your own way, you get to make some of the rules.

From college, I went right into my first real-world job . . . for a very conservative organization. Uh-oh. The fact that I was, shall we say, *fey*, couldn't be hidden. Since I was a writer who worked in corporate communications, we got a pass of sorts for being quirky and different—"Oh, those 'creatives!'" Even so, it was all very "don't ask, don't tell." It was telegraphed to me in numerous ways that there was only so much about me my employer wanted to know.

For this job I had moved from small-town Tennessee (albeit a progressive small town) to Atlanta, the San Francisco of the Southeast. I could essentially have a gay life and a work life, and the place was big enough so the twain never had to meet. Remember, this was before the Internet and everyone being able to find out anything they wanted to know about anyone. Again, it seemed a small price to pay for being able to be me—at least some of the time.

WITH A MOVE TO Atlanta came an almost immediate love

connection. I had that "I'm home" feeling with John I had not experienced prior to our meeting. As happened all too often in the late eighties, one of the first things John told me about himself was that he was HIV-positive. There was no running from that or from him. I was hooked, I loved him, and if his HIV status came as part of the package, then so be it. We lived "on the moon," as author Paul Monette put it in his memoir *Borrowed Time*. Only our closest circle knew John's diagnosis and he liked it that way.

You know where this is headed. Love, or the death of love, or, more accurately, the death of my beloved, would eventually bring me to being out full-time. After all, it was the era of only one HIV pharmaceutical. Yes, John died. Because we had indeed been living on the moon, it surprised a lot of people when this vibrant twenty-eight-year-old man died rather suddenly. He died of AIDS-related cancer, so just plain "cancer" became the stated cause to those like my employer who couldn't—or didn't want to—know more. Keep in mind that many Southerners still whisper "cancer," much less "HIV" or "AIDS."

And, as much as I like to say that no one has those TV-movie-worthy epiphanies, I did have my own stark realization the morning John died: *nothing will ever be the same*. It wasn't, either, but not in sweeping, dramatic ways that were immediately apparent. This was sometimes a slow-as-molasses process, but a crucial one.

I began by telling my employer I would be out for a week. *I know I only have three days for funeral leave. Still, I've just found my "roommate" dead. See you in a week.* That might seem a small step to some, but it was a huge step for me. John meant the world to me and I was not going to let small-minded rules and regulations make me rush him into a rural Mississippi grave so I could get back to my desk.

Mind you, I didn't return to work in drag or even as fully "out," but I hid myself less and less. The game of omission, not saying quite everything, became acceptable to me. But I would no longer lie about crucial aspects of myself. Even if I wasn't always sure I owed myself that, I knew I owed it to John, to my love for him, and to what we had been together. Maybe I still wasn't sure that *I* wasn't shameful, but I knew *our love* had not been.

Minor coming out steps followed, especially during the settlement of John's estate. More than once I had to state what my relationship was to the "decedent," and I was glad to claim him as my partner, no matter the reaction on the other end of the phone.

THE NEXT BIG STEP came two years later when my best friend from college also died of AIDS. This time I told those at work and everywhere else just what had killed my fine friend Tony. By this time AIDS had claimed too many folks not to speak out. And maybe it was the harsh lesson I needed. If I allowed folks to intimidate me into staying quiet, how could I ever help sound the alarm about AIDS?

You might say that in 1993 times had changed and enough other people were out that it couldn't have been that difficult for me to come out. But it's never that easy. We all come out in our own ways in our own times and for our own reasons. Heck, we only come out to the degree to which it is comfortable for each of us.

It took AIDS to bring me out. Or at least it took AIDS taking the man I loved to finally make me want to take the risk of living life as me—the whole me. Even if the realization did not come as a romance-novel-worthy epiphany, it did bring an emotional reflection on my part. If we lived in a culture that wasn't so suppressive, one that had permitted us all to live more openly sooner, one that wasn't so overwhelmed with false religiosity, we would be much further along in the fight against AIDS.

Did the Modern Plague get a head start on us because we collectively allowed ourselves to be pushed back into the closet? Into the shadows? Into a place where we couldn't discuss ourselves and our health more openly? It may sound too philosophical for some, but I say it's worth considering. Especially in an era in which we still can't seem to get comfortable with openness. And, in an era in which AIDS is still winning.

If AIDS isn't enough of a jolt to bring about a collective epiphany, then what is? It brought me out, and from that, there is no turning back.

9.

The Gay Kids and
the Johns Committee

= Merril Mushroom =

I n 1956, when I was in my third year of high school, the terrors of McCarthyism came home to the lesbians and gay men of South Florida where I lived.

South Florida was a gay paradise in the '50s. I say "gay," not "gay and lesbian," because "gay" was how we all referred to ourselves. In those days, "lesbian" was a word spoken only in whispers, like "vagina." We all were "gay," and there were many of us—gay guys, gay girls, gay life, gay parties, gay restaurants, gay bars, gay beach. Homosexuality was a subject that was discussed openly. Even when I was in grade school, I'd often overhear adults talking about the "homos," and by the time I entered high school my friends and I were well aware that there were lots of homos living in Dade County, which included Miami Beach and the city of Miami. So I was not at all surprised to learn that several of my friends had been hanging out at the gay beach, and that some of them were even coming out; and, soon enough, so did I.

However, "gay" did not mean "okay," and despite the extent of our gay subculture and our numbers in the gay community, being gay was not acceptable, nor safe, nor legal. Straight people considered homosexuality to be an aberration, an inversion, a crime against nature, and the laws upheld this attitude. Lesbians and gay men could be and often were harassed, beaten up, arrested, and incarcerated in prisons or mental hospitals, simply for the crime of being who we were. And the reality of this danger was always with us. It lurked as a constant fear in our lives.

IN 1954, SEVERAL MOMENTOUS events took place:

The year before, Julius and Ethel Rosenberg, alleged Communist spies, had been executed here in the United States, and Americans were being brainwashed with fear about the communist threat to our way of life. In 1954, hearings led by Senator Joe McCarthy began as part of federal investigations into "un-American activities." The McCarthy hearings were designed to ferret out supposed communists among us using evidence obtained through blackmail, intimidation tactics, and other illegal means, and innocent American citizens were victimized in the process.

MERRIL MUSHROOM came out in the fifties as a bar dyke. Her writing has appeared over the years in a wide variety of anthologies and periodicals. Her stories about the fifties' bar scene in Florida were first published in *Common Lives/Lesbian*  *Lives* magazine, and she was a frequent contributor to early issues of *Maize* magazine. Her out-of-print lesbian sci-fi novel, *Daughters of Khaton*, is looking for a new home. She lives on a rural Tennessee hill farm and is grateful for her gardens, friends, families, and her activist life. She is a member of Womonwrites, OLOC, and several rural grassroots organizations. She is still the butch.

Coincidentally, in 1954 a gay man named Bill Simpson was murdered in Miami by a teenaged hustler. The case became sensationalized by the media, and the fact that Dade County had a large gay subculture was exposed. The outraged straight public demanded that something be done to purge the county of this pestilence—not the murder, but the gay subculture. An anti-crime commission was set up to investigate gambling, which was big business at the time, as well as "perversion," *i.e.*, homosexuality. Police began to raid gay bars and beaches and arrest citizens for questioning.

Perhaps the most important event of 1954 was that the U.S. Supreme Court ruled in the *Brown vs. Board of Education* case that racial segregation of public schools was unconstitutional. Over the next two years, as the McCarthy hearings continued to ruin people's lives, and gays in Dade County were forced to retreat deeper into their closets, confrontations around civil rights and integration of the nation's schools were erupting with increasing frequency throughout the South.

In 1956, the Florida legislature, hoping to prevent violence around race relations in segregationist Florida, appointed a committee chaired by State Representative Henry Hand to monitor civil rights organizations. Unfortunately, the committee soon fell to the control of State Senator Charlie Johns, a staunch segregationist who was outspokenly homophobic. An admirer of Joe McCarthy and his techniques, Johns redefined the committee to fit the McCarthy template, focusing on exposing the communists he thought were instigating civil rights activities. He called for investigations of civil rights organizations, socialists, anti-nuclear and peace activists, and, especially, members of the NAACP, which Johns considered to be the main communist front organization. The Florida Legislative Investigative Committee—now known as "the Johns Committee"—began to hold hearings during which members questioned blacks about their association with the NAACP and other "intergrationist" groups. But the NAACP, led by the Reverend Theodore Gibson of Miami, successfully challenged the constitutionality of the committee's demands in court. Johns, frustrated in his attempts to intimidate Miami blacks, turned his sights on a new and completely vulnerable target—the "homosexual menace."

Then, with the state encouraging city and county law enforcement, raids on the gay bars and beach increased dramatically, and many more citizens were arrested. Local newspapers fell on this information like hyenas, publishing lists with names, addresses, telephone numbers, and places of employment of the "perverts" and front-page articles denouncing the freaks of nature who were taking over Miami Beach.

Meanwhile, I had graduated from high school and was attending the University of Florida in Gainesville. I had several gay friends at school, and I frequented the gay clubs and beach when I was home. Sometimes, I'd be in one of my favorite nightclubs, dancing, conversing, or just sitting on my bar stool, when the music suddenly would stop and the lights would go on, signifying a police raid. We'd immediately cease all same-sex contact of any kind and grab someone of the opposite sex to pretend we were with. The fear and tension was palpable, because one never really knew what the police might do. Usually, the owners of the club would step aside with them, money would exchange hands, and the boys in blue would leave. But sometimes they would come among us, check our identification, make lewd comments over the contents of our wallets, and take great pleasure in insulting us. Leering at attractive femmes, they would engage in inappropriate touching, while spewing lesbian-bashing diatribes. They always harassed the butches and queens most of all, arresting and taking them to the police station where they were physically inspected to determine if they were wearing three articles of sex-appropriate clothing as required by law. If they were not—or, sometimes, even if they were—they were thrown into a jail cell to await charges, which might or might not be brought.

The gay beach was similarly raided, but there was no one on the beach to provide a payoff. That beach was a wonderful gathering place—a block-long stretch of sand and surf teeming with gay girls and gay guys, bounded by a small hotel on one side and a long pavilion with a snack bar on the other. There was a juke box on the pavilion, and we'd dance to its music down the length of the concrete jetty, out over the Atlantic, to six plays for a quarter: lindy, bop, foxtrot, samba, hully-gully, and cha-cha-cha. We'd dance mixed-sex, gay girls with gay guys, so that we wouldn't be arrested and charged with "crimes against nature" by the many undercover police who haunted the beach like vultures.

But sometimes we would suddenly, unexpectedly, be approached by officers, grabbed, and pushed roughly toward the sidewalk. Sometimes, as we lay on our towels and blankets, sat on our chairs and chaise lounges, floated in the ocean on our rafts and inner tubes, we'd be assaulted by an onslaught of uniformed police and plainclothes agents, ordered to our feet, and marched from the beach. We'd be loaded into waiting paddy wagons, gay girls and gay guys together, and taken to the local police station. There we were booked and fingerprinted and locked in cells, sometimes beaten, humiliated, sexually assaulted, other times not. You just never knew what was in store. How dare we filth have the nerve to swim, sun, eat, and enjoy ourselves on a public beach?

With what am I being charged, officer?

Vagrancy.

Vagrancy? But I have a job, a home, a family, a reputation in the community. I have money and identification in my wallet. I was only sunbathing on a public beach on a weekend. I am not a vagrant.

We have twenty-seven different counts of vagrancy we can charge you with. We can book you and put you in a jail cell and hold you for twenty-four hours on suspicion. We can do with you as we please, you filthy queer!

AS THE RAIDS ON the bars, the beach, and even private parties became routine, the Johns Committee investigators concentrated their attention on schools in the state, especially the universities, which they considered to be hotbeds of radicalism, "intergrationism," and homosexuality. At the private University of Miami, the administration refused to allow investigators on campus; but the administrators of the public universities—the University of Florida in Gainesville and Florida State University in Tallahassee—chose to welcome and assist the investigators.

Paid informants infiltrated sorority and fraternity houses, intent on finding and exposing the queers. Rooms in the local motels were bugged with recording devices. Plainclothes police lurked in the public bathrooms that were reputed to be homosexual meeting places, encouraging overtures from gay men, then arresting them and forcing them to name others. Private detectives followed suspected homosexuals, noting where they went and with whom they associated. The investigators maintained lengthy files on the personal lives of their victims. They harassed, threatened, intimidated, and blackmailed gay men and lesbians into turning in their friends. Eventually, the scope of the investigations broadened to include teachers in the Florida public schools.

In 1959, information that had been amassed during the investigations was organized to be presented during secret hearings under the control of Investigator R. J. Strickland. These hearings were scheduled to begin at the state universities after classes resumed in the fall, and this fact was circulated through our grapevine amid terrifying rumors and speculation.

All of us gay college kids knew people who had been arrested, but we did not know if they'd broken down and named others. No one knew who exactly might have been implicated, but we all were vulnerable. We all were afraid that any of us might have been on the list of those accused, and our anxiety escalated as fall approached. Our greatest fears were that we'd be exposed, kicked out of school, labeled forever as a pervert, and, for some of us, that our parents would find out. Always, there was the threat of incarceration in jail or the mental hospital. We'd wonder in conversation among ourselves: *Well, Artie was busted. Did that mean he'd named Elliot? He said he hadn't, but what if he really had? If Elliot was called in, would he name Sandra and Kerry? Kerry had a big mouth. Would he expose the rest of us to save his own skin?*

We soon would find out.

Armed with tape recordings, photographs, letters and other documents, and the testimonies of paid informers and surveillance witnesses, the committee convened and began pulling in the victims. One by one, gays who had been entrapped were called before the panel of judges and interrogated as to their private lives and personal friends. They were intimidated, verbally abused, emotionally bludgeoned and threatened in the panel's attempts to pressure them to name other gays. And when they did, immediately upon exposure, lesbian and gay university professors, administrators, and public school teachers were dismissed from their jobs and publicly humiliated. Many others, both gay and straight, resigned out of fear or in protest.

Then the investigators went after the college students. Sometimes gay students, too young to be experienced in handling such harassment, were given a choice—they could be expelled from school and exposed as a homosexual, or they could go into psychiatric treatment to be "cured." One by one, my friends began to fall.

In 1959, Penny was kicked out of school. Despite having a statement signed by all the girls in her dormitory that she had never tried to touch them, the dean of women said she posed too much of a danger to remain. Harry refused to see a psychiatrist, had the audacity to insist that he was not sick, and was expelled. Leo's parents had him committed to the state mental hospital when they learned that he was gay. Jennifer was permitted to remain in school as long as she kept her weekly appointments with the psychologist, but she was not allowed to live in the dormitory and had to commute from a room off-campus.

MY OWN TURN CAME toward the end of the semester. I was called in for questioning in the basement of my dormitory by a detective. I didn't think that I had been named before the committee, but evidently I had been seen with gays on the social scene, not on campus in Gainesville, but in Tampa, where, thinking I would be safe, I went to the gay bars—and it was about my Tampa friends that I was questioned. Despite my terror, I contrived a story to try to convince the detective that I was straight—that my BOYfriend and I associated with these particular gays because they knew how much we loved each other, so they let us meet at their house, because there was nowhere else we could go to be together. In my fear, I began to weep, and through my sobs, I begged the detective not to get my friends or my BOYfriend into trouble, because my gay friends were only trying to help me and my BOYfriend. The detective watched me for a moment. Then he leaned close to me. "Well," he said, his voice smooth, "what about here on campus?"

"Huh?"

"If you're friendly with, um, homos, then you must know who they are here on campus, right?"

My head began to spin. I was out of the frying pan and into the conflagration. "No!" I lied desperately. "I don't know any homos here. My friends in Tampa just happen to be . . . that way. They were so nice to let me and my BOYfriend stay at their house. Please don't get my friends or my BOYfriend into trouble. My BOYfriend and I are so in love, and we're planning to get married."

"Hum, well," he bent down and put his arm around my shoulders, spoke in soft, conspiratorial tones, "if you get along with, um, gays . . . well, you could find out who they are here on campus, right? They would trust you, right?"

"I don't understand what you mean," I sobbed, trying not to

cringe away from his touch. Unfortunately, I understood what he meant all too well.

"My dear little lady," he said, "you may not understand, but these are very sick people. Even your friends, although you may not realize it, need our help. Homosexuality is a disease." He shook his head, a grimace of pity mixed with disgust on his face.

"Help them?" Behind the total nastiness of what this man was suggesting that I do, I felt a strange, cold joy rising through me, as I realized, *My God! He believes me! He has swallowed my boyfriend story! Oh, thank goodness! He doesn't think I'm a queer!*

"Yes," he was saying, "They need to see a psychiatrist, and if that doesn't cure them, they need more aggressive treatment. If you really care about them, if these people truly are your friends, then you'll help us to reach them so we can see that they get help." He stood up. "Now you go think about this, think about it very seriously, and I will get back in touch with you."

"Okay." I nearly ran out of the basement, fled back to my room. There, I thought very seriously, as he'd suggested, but not about informing on my friends, but about how I could convince my mamma—who knew nothing about any of this, not even that I was gay—to let me change schools, to leave the state university where tuition was cheap and transfer to the University of Miami where I could finish my education in safety. The semester was almost over. I could stall, promise the detective I'd work with him when the new semester began. Meanwhile, all I wanted right now was to get the hell out of Dodge.

IN THE END, I was one of the more fortunate survivors of the Johns Investigations. Not so, many others: In Miami, a high school teacher sealed his apartment and turned on the jets of his gas stove. A businessman whose name appeared on one of the newspaper lists of perverts took an overdose of sleeping pills. A seventeen-year-old girl hanged herself from a tree in her back yard with the sash of a terrycloth bathrobe. And a young gay man, in his terror over being exposed as a queer, jumped from the second floor of the Miami police station and fatally impaled himself on the decorative iron fence that surrounded the building like a row of spears.

I transferred to the University of Miami that fall, and the detective did not follow me. In 1962, I graduated and moved to Alabama for a year, then to New York City where I lived for the next decade. I remember my amazement when, shortly after I arrived in New York, I was caught in a raid on a gay bar. Unlike Florida raids, where we might have been arrested, the police simply sent all the patrons outside and closed the bar for the night.

Meanwhile, in the South, violence around civil rights continued, the U.S. entered into war with Vietnam, and Senator Charlie Johns added "communistic ideas" back onto his purge agenda and intensified investigations of homosexuals. His heavy-handed tactics finally began to alienate people, and he resigned as chairman of the committee, but he continued to influence its functioning.

In 1964, the Johns Committee published a report: *Homosexuality and Citizenship in Florida*. Known as "The Purple Pamphlet" because of the color of its cover, this hate-filled homophobic document contained a wealth of inflammatory misinformation, was liberally illustrated with lascivious photographs, and outlined a recommended "Homosexual Practices Control Act for Florida," with detailed penalties for anyone who engaged in such crimes against nature. The forty-four-page booklet was printed and distributed at taxpayer expense to legislators, state officials, and the news media. The pamphlet was so over the top that it actually offended most of the people it was intended to convince, creating an uproar of disapproval over the actions of the committee. Still, the investigations continued, with State Attorney Richard Gerstein promising further crackdowns on Florida perverts.

That summer, a hero arose. Richard A. Inman, a gay taxi driver, fed up with nine years of oppression from the Johns Committee, formed a state chartered corporation, the Atheneum Society of America, whose objective was, as noted in James T. Sears's *Lonely Hunters: An Oral History of Lesbian and Gay Southern Life, 1948–1968,* was "to combat . . . gross injustices affecting homosexual citizens which are perpetuated by certain heterosexuals who masquerade behind the guise of 'justice' and 'decency.'"

Inman and the Atheneum Society joined forces with the ACLU and other groups working for legislative and religious reform. Highly visible and outspoken, Inman threatened Dade County with a lawsuit. He threatened the city of Miami Beach with a blatantly gay parade at the height of the tourist season. He made speeches, wrote letters, lobbied legislators, and took on Charlie Johns and Richard Gerstein.

Through patience, perseverance, and the masterful use of political dialectics, Inman became increasingly influential. Finally, the Florida legislature simply discontinued funding for the Johns Committee, and that was the end of it. The climate of fear and oppression, however, continued unabated until 1969 when the demonstrations at the Stonewall bar in New York City heralded a new day. The beginning of the Gay Pride movement was born.

10.

The Approximate Weight of Truth

= SUZANNE LEA =

D uring the summers of my childhood, a good, flat skipping stone was as precious and valuable as currency. My cousins and I spent hours along the banks of the creek that ran behind our house, searching for the perfect vehicle on which to transport tall tales—five skips, seven skips, ten skips—a stone that would float across the mirrored surface of the Tennessee River touching gently, creating echoes of echoes of tiny waves. At about seven or eight years old, I began having a recurring dream. I dreamed that I had one of those river stones hidden inside my mouth. But, the dream-stone that slept inside my mouth at night was as bitter as shame and twice as sharp.

Over the years, the circumstances of the dream varied, but the stone was always the same. Night after night, I would drift, the stone pressed firmly against the roof of my mouth. I would run my tongue along its flat body, exploring its grainy surface and jagged edges. And I would wake each morning, my mouth sore and raw, lips bloodied from silently protecting my stone.

I lived half my life with a secret, dreamed half my dreams with that stone hidden inside my mouth. Then one day, I turned to speak and, without warning, the stone fell out. I offered its truth, rubbed nearly smooth after so many years, to my husband. "*I am sorry,*" I said. "*I am sorry for the lies I never meant to tell. I have fallen in love with a woman and my heart can barely contain the enormity of it.*" My husband examined my truth, holding it up to the sunlight, considering it carefully. "*I recognize this stone,*" he said. "*And the truth it tells. I've seen it in your restlessness. I've heard it behind your words. I've tasted it, bitter and lonely, inside your mouth. I love you, but this truth is yours and I cannot carry it for you.*"

So, I put the stone in my pocket and set out for love—twelve hundred miles and more. We made a home near the city, this inquisitive woman and I. We cooked and planted and traveled together. We loved fiercely, fought bitterly, and forgave easily. We built fires in winter and planted roses in the spring. Together we learned to make bread. Still, no matter how I tried to rewrite myself, my roots remained fixed in the warm, rich soil of Alabama. Always, the slow rhythm of the South pulled at me like the weight of the moon against the tide.

I loved her and I loved the city. I loved her certain hands, loved the noisy nights, the colors and the smells and the

---

SUZANNE LEA was born and raised in Alabama. Always believing herself to be an outsider, she imagined that a better-fitting life must surely exist someplace else. She moved to upstate New York to live with her lover, where they worked in a bio-organic farming community. Missing family, home, history, and the rhythms of the South, she returned and now lives and works in Atlanta. Suzanne has regularly contributed to *The Alabama Free Press* (TAF Press) and the (now out of print) *Sinister Compendium*.

distractions of us. But, I simply could not forget the feel of red mud and riverbanks, stained feet on summer days. I missed the rhythm of the South, so like a heartbeat . . . so like my heartbeat. Alabama was not her home, but because she loved me, she understood that it was mine and she released me, back to myself.

Surprised to discover that I was ready to travel alone, I packed my car and began the long drive home. Somewhere along the Taconic Highway, on a path that borders a field of statues, bits of granite set free to grow into the shapes of larger things, I realized I couldn't carry my river stone another step. So, I buried it and took up the truth instead. Placed it gently on the tip of my tongue, closed my mouth around it and walked away. Walked away from the city, but not away from myself. I understood, finally, that even without her, I am as queer as my dreams of the secret stone. It has been many years since leaving, many years since my return, and many years since I've tasted the shame of that secret. On occasion, though, I can still recall with perfect clarity the exact shape and texture, taste and sharpness of it. But, it is its weight that I recall most vividly—its weight, which in my recollection is the approximate weight of truth.

11.

The Other Side of the Net

≡ SUSAN L. BENTON ≡

I t was a Thursday night three weeks into my sophomore year at a small Alabama liberal arts college. The hot muggy weather was melting away, and there was the promise of a beautiful autumn in the air. It should have been a wonderfully happy evening, but I was anxious—there were ominous signs that things were not as they should be. Although I wouldn't know it for another few days, my life was about to be turned upside down.

I had been a lonely child. Both my parents were only children, and as the firstborn I was raised to be independent and self-sufficient, becoming a little adult long before my time. I usually had only one good friend and if something happened, such as when my best friend in fourth and fifth grades suddenly moved to Louisiana, I was alone for the rest of the school year. I had skipped a grade early in my school years and so was always the youngest in my class. My parents were supportive of my musical and intellectual talents, but they couldn't help me with the fact that making friends my own age was a challenge. I was more comfortable with adults or with very young children. If I ever belonged, it was with the nerdy pack—the honor society kids—or with the musicians. My mother admitted that my high school geometry teacher told her that even though I was the youngest student she had ever taught, I was one of the most gifted students in her class, and one of the most socially inept.

When I finally left home in the early seventies to go to college (albeit only on the other side of my Alabama hometown), I decided I wanted to "belong," and so I signed up to go through sorority rush. I figured out that there was a pecking order to the sororities—the rich girls pledged this one, the jocks pledged that one, the misfits pledged yet another. Foolish me: I wanted the rich girls to pick me, but I ended up with the scholars again.

I was ecstatically happy as a sorority girl. I finally had a group of "sisters" who loved me just as I was. We used a very Southern convention and spoke about each other as being "of the bolt," meaning that we were cut from the same cloth. I finally belonged.

I HAD DISCOVERED THE word for what I was when I was fifteen. Although I can honestly say in hindsight that I fell in love with my first "older woman" when I was nine, I had had numerous crushes on girls and women: on female schoolteachers, a female pediatrician at my church, girls at summer camp, and older girls in high school. I have no idea whether the copy of *Everything You Always Wanted to Know About Sex: But Were Afraid to Ask* (high on the bookshelf in the junk room) was meant for me to find, or whether my poor confused-about-her-daughter's-life mother had gotten it as a reference book for herself. In any case, finding the word "lesbian" (after struggling with "tribad" and "invert") was exciting and reassuring. There *were* other women who felt like I did. I immediately started looking for them.

I came out in the physical sense the summer before college. I was seventeen and my first lover was twenty-five. She took me to bed in a house borrowed for the weekend. I remember the first time I saw her come through the door of the office where I had taken a summer job. I swear the sun rose in the sky and the orchestra started playing. I was smitten, and she was scared. After all, I was still jail bait! But she showed me what I wanted to know, gently and passionately.

I knew enough to keep quiet and, above all, to divert suspicion. A strict family background, coupled with immersion in Southern Bible-Belt Protestant church society in the late fifties and sixties had taught me there were some things I needed to hide. We Southerners instinctively knew to protect family skeletons, even if we might have been curiously proud of them. We were taught to be stoic and hide our feelings. Given my

SUSAN L. BENTON was born in Germany as an "Army brat," but was raised in Alabama. She graduated from college with a major in music education and worked as a preschool teacher and church musician. Seduced by the lucrative profession of computer programming and escaping Alabama, she received an MBA in information systems from Boston University. Susan relocated to Hong Kong where she worked for a global accounting firm. Susan and her spouse, who is Australian, were among the first post-DOMA Green Card applicants— a process that took more than a year to complete. She might sound like a Yankee (or an Aussie) every once in a while, but underneath it all, she's still a Southern lady.

Linda J. Nelson

B. Docktor

childhood need for love and approval, my early feelings for other girls felt wrong and were carefully hidden.

NOW I WAS IN college and just two months in I realized that I had fallen in love with Pat,* one of my sorority sisters, and she with me. We were as discreet as we could be in a dormitory situation, but it turned out that our attitudes about being lesbians were quite different; she was bolder than I. In the spring semester of my freshman year—Pat's senior year—when directly questioned by a suspicious sorority sister, she revealed our relationship. With only two months left until she graduated she had little to lose by being honest. I had the rest of my college life ahead of me, and she had "outed" me long before I was ready.

However, I was elected Rush Chairman, an unprecedented honor for a freshman. It seemed the sorority had decided I was okay after all. By the beginning of my sophomore year, after a summer away, I had begun to relax a little. We'd gone through a successful Rush Week and pledged our quota.

Two weeks after rush was over each new pledge was assigned a Big Sister and today was the day of the event—Big Sisters were to be announced. I had developed a friendship with two of the new pledges; in fact, both had told me that they had pledged because of me. One of the pledges, Jessie, was to be my Little Sister. Our names had been paired at the meeting of the Big Sister committee, of which I was a member, the night before. I was ecstatic. Jessie had put me down as her first choice!

About two that afternoon, there was a knock on my door. Several of the sorority officers came into my room and informed me that I was not going to be given a Little Sister. I

---

*The writer has fictionalized the names of her sorority sisters to protect their privacy.

was shocked and pressed them for a reason. Hemming and hawing, one officer told me that since I had had trouble with my grades the previous year they didn't think it wise for me to have a Little Sis. I'd had mononucleosis my first term and definitely had grade problems with an abstract math course. But I had taken a full load during the summer term to catch up, and I had a 3.5 GPA.

I realized the reason they were giving was bogus and called them on it. One of the officers finally admitted that it was because I was a lesbian. Jessie was to be paired with Meg, the only remaining sorority member without a Little Sister. And they didn't want any trouble from me about their decision. I knew Jessie had already expressed a distinct dislike of Meg. I also had a reason to dislike Meg. She was the person who had confronted Pat about our relationship, and she had taken her knowledge all the way up the chain of command. Our Second Vice President, the head of what was called the Standards Board, had told her to shut up and leave us alone. So Meg had gone to the Dean of Housing, and finally to the Dean of Students, where she was, at least on the surface, ignored. But the irony was that Meg had also been in love with Pat. It had been clear to me, and to Pat, in the way that Meg had always tried to sit next to Pat in our sorority suite, in the way she looked at Pat, and in how she vied for Pat's attention. And now, she was to get *my* Little Sis.

I was in shock for a few minutes after they left, but then I got angry. Any hesitations I might have had about "coming out" to a younger woman were consumed by my anger at the unfairness of it all. Without any fears or qualms, I marched myself down to Jessie's room, and luckily found her there. I told her exactly what had happened—that I had wanted her for my Little Sister and I knew I was her first choice as well.

The reason I would not be able to be her Big Sis was that I was gay and the sorority felt it was not appropriate. My need for honesty outweighed any consequences, anticipated or not, of my confession. I'll never forget Jessie's response. She said she didn't care what I was, I would always be her Big Sis.

And then someone knocked on her door. Jessie opened it to the same group of women who had stood at my door thirty minutes earlier. They were there to tell her that she would not be getting her first choice (or *any* of her choices) of Big Sister. I must admit, I relished the look of surprise on their faces when they saw me in Jessie's room. Perhaps they had underestimated me.

I WENT THROUGH THE motions that night. Each pledge found out who her Big Sister would be. In fact, it was one of the most historic nights in women's history—Thursday night, September 20, 1973, the night that Billie Jean King beat Bobby Riggs in tennis. As my whole sorority crowded into one of the suite living rooms to watch the match, I sat with my anger, my disappointment, my loneliness and my growing anxiety that something was really wrong here.

The end of my young world, as I then knew it, came three nights later on Sunday night. I was ordered to report to the Chapter House for an eight p.m. meeting. With my heart beating wildly, I answered the summons, walking down the hill to the Chapter House, alone, in the dark.

There were not many people there. The first vice president and several other officers were seated in a formal meeting arrangement. Without much fanfare, they announced that they wanted me to resign from the sorority on moral charges. And they let me know in no uncertain terms that if I did not resign, they would make my life very difficult through "exposure" to the whole college community.

I tried to bargain. I said I would transfer to another college that didn't have a chapter or one with no sororities at all. No dice. I asked why I was being forced to resign when last year's president of the chapter had been openly sleeping with her boyfriend and several other sisters smoked dope. Deaf ears. I'm not sure if it was that night or later that someone finally revealed that it was the alumni association that was making such a fuss. They were deathly afraid that the chapter would fold if lesbianism were even whispered about within the sorority, much less known to the campus as a whole.

I don't remember how I got back to my room. Soon after getting there, my own Big Sister came to me. She said she had not been told of any of this and that she was mad as hell. She bundled me up and told me she was taking me home to my parents. Like a babe, I followed her blindly to her vintage Mercedes (funny what we remember!) and let her drive me home.

Going home with this news could have been a lot more painful than it was, but the day before I had moved back to campus at the start of the school year, my long-suspecting mother had finally put the question of my being a lesbian out in the open. At two in the morning, as I stuffed the final box into my car, she had asked me to sit down and point blank said to me, "I want to know how far you are into homosexuality."

Talk about having a heart attack! I remember my answer— or my attempt at an answer as I muttered, "Well, I have some friends who are gay . . ." My mother wasn't buying it. She retorted, "I don't want to know about your friends. I want to know about you."

My reaction was to burst into tears. I sat frozen on the couch, crying buckets. I wasn't yet ready to face the world with who I was, much less my parents. The positive aspect of having her force the information out of me at least meant she was not in for a complete shock when Alexis brought me home a mere three weeks later.

I don't remember if I stayed the night at my parents' home or if Alexis took me back to school. What I do remember is Alexis's anger at the sorority for keeping all of this from her as well as my mother's righteous indignation that they would do this to *her* daughter. Though I was totally devastated, I did take strength and comfort in their support.

The next day I snuck around campus, trying to get to my classes, while avoiding members of the sorority. But, as I was heading back up the hill from my classes to the dorm quad, I saw all the sororities on the slope, preparing for their group pictures for the yearbook. I was supposed to have been with them. My eyes flooded with tears, and I ran to my room, threw myself on my bed, and cried throughout the evening.

DURING THE NEXT TWO days, every time I went into the college cafeteria, I saw hands flutter to faces and heard the whispering going on. I tried to sit at the sorority table and was told I was not welcome. And, with this continuing rejection, I began to get more and more angry.

Anger can be a positive force when one is depressed, and when I kicked into action, I took up the sword of anger with a vengeance. I contacted the sports team leader of Gamma Delta Iota (GDI—or God-Damned Independents, a rabid anti-sorority group) and said I was available for their volleyball team. As one of the sorority's leading athletes, my joining was not only great for me, but the GDIs scored a real coup in getting me.

One week after being denied a Little Sister and four days after being kicked out of my sorority, I faced my former "sisters" on the other side of the net in a crucial volleyball game.

The God-Damned Independents won the match and I began my healing process.

I stayed at the college and did my best to come through the trauma. Since I hid either in the Music Building or in my room I earned a 4.0 that semester. One of the more humorous things to come from this time was a comment made by my grandmother. She knew something was wrong with me and she could tell my parents were terribly upset, but for the life of her, she couldn't quite figure out what was going on. Based on her scanty knowledge of modern young people, she suggested to my mother that maybe I was on drugs. My mother's response was quick, though not particularly enlightening, noting only that she didn't think I would be pulling off a 4.0 average if I were caught up in that "mess."

While she has been loving throughout my life, I have always carried the burden of knowing that my mother hates the fact that I am a lesbian. I was a perfect child, "except . . ."

I CAN HONESTLY SAY that I still cry when I remember this time, even though it has been nearly thirty-five years. Several of my so-called "sisters," including the one who took her knowledge to the Dean of Students and was rebuffed, went to other colleges throughout Alabama to hold "purges" in chapter houses. Pledges in my chapter were told to get boyfriends.

I recently reconnected with a former "sister" who was in my sorority chapter, and she shared that she was aware that she was a lesbian at the time. She told of her own fears of being "discovered" and how frightening "the inquisition" was to other closeted lesbians. She felt guilty in not coming to my defense, but of course she would have been thrown out, too. She wanted my forgiveness, but I told her she needed none. I had been on her side of the net—scared of the same "discovery." In many ways, I think I had it easier. I was "out"—perhaps not proud, but at least I didn't have to hide it anymore.

I held my head high throughout the next three years, graduating with honors and becoming the first woman to win the college's highest citizenship award. Less than half of my pledge class stayed with the sorority through the full four years of college, and I was the only one from my year to distinguish myself academically. Still, nothing has ever seemed as sweet as winning that volleyball game on the other side of the net.

12.

Straight as Florida's Turnpike

⇒ STEPHANIE WOOLLEY-LARREA ⇐

"I'm going to marry a boy. Is that okay?" my five-year-old daughter Anais asked as we were driving to yet another birthday party in the plethora of birthday parties that is childhood. Driving is where we have our best conversations.

"Of course it's okay," I said, realizing exactly how backwards this conversation sounded, how someone outside this car, outside of our life, would perceive it.

"You can marry anyone you want," I said, "as long as they're nice to you."

"I want to marry a sister!" said my son, Jacob, with glee.

"Well, that's the one rule. You can't marry anyone in your family."

"Okay," he said, and I'm glad he doesn't ask why.

They are all five years old, my three children, and we have talked openly about many topics, but I have stopped short of talking about sex. We're operating under a "don't ask, don't tell" policy, although I think my reasons are more sensible than Bill Clinton's were. This is not about keeping secrets; children ask questions about what they're ready to hear, and until they ask, I'm going to assume they're not ready. Right now, all they think you need for a marriage is love, and that's good enough.

"When you weren't married to Mami," Emma said, "did you know you wanted to marry a girl?"

"Yes," I said. As if it were that simple.

"And then you met Mami and she was the girl for you!"

"Exactly," I said.

I'm happy to leave such an easy narrative in her head. Truthfully, though, my coming-out story isn't wrought with the same sort of pain, rejection, and stigma as many of those who came out before me. Because, of course, those men and women paved the way. Girls like me, who came out in the early 1990s, were cresting the wave of the lesbian trend. (Although my first real girlfriend shuddered every time I called any female over eighteen a girl, we were girls, naïve and fresh.) We came out with Melissa and k.d. and the Indigo Girls. There were movies about us at the theater and shows about us on television. We were lucky.

I was as shocked as the rest of my family when I fell in love with a college dorm mate. But I wasn't *shocking*, and that made my transition significantly easier.

An English major, I set about confirming my identity with books, most of which focused on coming out, not what came later. My pages of *Rubyfruit Jungle*—set at my university's rival, only two hours south—were well-loved and dog-eared. *Spring Forward, Fall Back*, written by one of my university's professors, was also much read (and now autographed).

IT'S AN OLD AND volatile argument: whether being gay is a choice or not. I do think it's a choice—between following your feelings or ignoring them. To do the latter is to limit your happiness; it's not to doom you to a life of misery, but it would cap the ceiling on how much love you could give and receive, and while not tragic in the true sense of that word, sad nonetheless.

I'm sure someone somewhere has patterned the stages of coming out after the stages of grief: denial, anger, bargaining, depression, then acceptance. For me, denial was first and foremost, not because I wanted to deny myself happiness, but because I was afraid that in accepting the feelings I had for other women as lifelong, I would be denying myself the other thing I wanted so badly: motherhood.

As part of my bargaining phase, which might have been actually a subset of denial, I called a former boyfriend: sweet, safe and loyal. We tried dating again, playing with the fantasy future he had created for us in high school: marriage and kids. After a few months though, I knew two things: if I had to marry a man, it would be him, but I did not want to marry a man. It was truly a case of "it's not you, it's me," and seventeen years later, we are still friends, and I think he finally understands.

STEPHANIE WOOLLEY-LARREA was born in North Carolina but migrated to Miami where she continues to live with her wife of many years and their triplets. An English teacher and aspiring novelist, she has made it a goal never to back away from educating others about acceptance, which she considers much more important than tolerance. She holds a bachelor's in English literature and a master's in creative writing. Her work has been published in *Sentence, Coe Review, Mipo, Florida English,* and  elsewhere. Of all her accomplishments, she is most proud of her children, who inspire her every day to be brave.

Amy Duffing

SIX MONTHS. IT WAS six months between the moment I realized I was in love with a woman and the moment I was able to say the words "I am a lesbian" without irony or tears. It was then that I set out to find my true lesbian identity. This was my real adolescence, not those pubescent junior high years spent playing with makeup and deodorant. I tried on personalities the way Barbie goes through outfits.

I tried on Nature Lesbian: bought some hiking boots, some flannel shirts, and a sleeping bag. I went on a Womyn Warrior nature hike one Saturday through the sinkholes, a favorite walking spot for those interested in both nature and random holes in the ground, and met a couple named Fran and Mary. Mary was a firefighter. Fran was pregnant. I must have seemed like a goofy puppy, following them through the path, watching Mary help Fran walk through the not very rugged terrain, asking a zillion and a half questions about their pregnancy. To me, they were a vision of my possible future. But my turn as Nature Lesbian was short lived. Turns out, I'm not a big fan of bugs or sweat.

I tried on Activist Lesbian. There are videotapes of me protesting something on the steps of a fraternity house at FSU. There are pictures of me at a Take Back the Night march down the center of campus. While I respect the women who deeply felt their convictions and had the energy and inclination to be angry enough to fight these things, mine was only camouflage anger, put on to fit in. Becoming a lesbian was about me being who I truly was: I didn't have to pretend anymore.

I tried on Intellectual Lesbian, seeking out movies and literature with gay themes and dissecting them using all my English Major tools. Eventually, though, I got tired of hearing myself talk.

Ultimately I went back to being myself, the who-I-was before

I added the tag of "lesbian" to my descriptors. Only this time, I didn't feel obligated to say yes when a man asked me on a date, which was the liberation I had been searching for.

By the time I graduated college, I had reached acceptance: I was many things: a writer, a reader, a teacher, and also a lesbian.

I wasn't finished adding all my adjectives, but I was on my way.

DURING MY TOUR OF Lesbian Personalities, I did find something I was looking for: community. Tallahassee, at that time, was one-third university, one-third government, and in that remaining third was an assortment of former Miss Watermelon contestants, aspiring folk musicians, Southern Baptists, and furloughed hippies.

I found my place somewhere between the musicians and the hippies, attending and performing at poetry readings, going to my first lesbian commitment ceremony (they registered for Fiesta Ware), singing along in concerts at dive bars. I was on-and-off single the second half of college, but I had a great social life regardless, mostly other lesbians, both veteran and rookie.

I'd always had friends: this was not the Ugly Duckling story or its modernized romantic-comedy-makeover story where someone slapped a pair of Doc Martens and nice-fitting jeans on me and suddenly I'm the Lesbian Prom Queen. This was more subtle and more fulfilling; I was part of a crowd, which had never happened previously. I spent my early adolescence being on the periphery of many crowds: the nerds, the burn-outs, the service geeks, the literary magazine editors, the swim team, the cheerleaders. I had a social life, but never a clique, never a group against which to measure myself, never a place to immediately belong.

In the magnolia- and patchouli-dripped roads of Tallahassee,

I fit in. My adolescence ended, and I became an adult.

Then I had to leave.

Graduation, while possible to postpone, is inevitable. Having a bachelor's in English wasn't going to get me too far, but I did have a Florida teaching certificate. As in many small towns where there is also a decent teacher-education program, there were no jobs available. That left me with two options: return home to Miami, or seek out a Florida town where I knew no one.

I WENT HOME, BACK to what I knew, back to my family, back into my career. I slowly came out to a few co-workers, with no rejection. However, I said nothing to my students, those pre-pubescent bundles of nerves. When I was eleven and twelve, I still wanted to believe my teachers slept in their classrooms at the end of the day: I didn't want to share my vision of them with any sort of imagined home life. I stopped short of lying to them, but I did use generic and gender-neutral pronouns if pressed: "We went to the art festival. I saw that movie." Regardless of my sexuality, I wanted to keep my private life private from them; it protected us all.

Homophobia remained something I saw on the news. I was grateful for that, but not immune to the great irony of Miami, a mostly blue city in a mostly red state, a school board that would give me domestic partner health benefits in a state where it was illegal to adopt children because of my homosexuality. Miami wasn't my first choice for a place to live for those reasons, but at the time, it was the easiest. Sometimes "by default" is the only way to make a choice.

Maybe subconsciously I knew I had other struggles ahead. Not in romance—in 1996, I met Mary and we easily became a part of each other's lives. Two years after we met, we began what became an arduous process of trying to make babies.

In addition to the actual physical resistance our bodies had to the baby-making process—four miscarriages in as many years—we had to prepare lots of answers for well-intended, but poorly informed family and friends who questioned the wisdom of bringing children into a homosexual home. Your children will be gay (if only gay people have gay children, how did I get here?), your children will be different (all children are different), people will look at you funny (so what?). We soldiered on on every front—through the world of infertility and among a crowd of friends, mostly straight, also starting families.

During that same period, the WNBA, the Women's National Basketball Association, formed. Miami got a team—the Sol. Previous to the arrival of the WNBA, I had absolutely no concept of what it meant to be a sports fan nor little concept of the game of basketball (something about an orange ball and two baskets). But the WNBA came, and so did the women. I honestly enjoyed the games, so much so that during away games I'd follow the radio play-by-play, my first occasion to use the AM dial. I also enjoyed the camaraderie: the bleachers were not completely packed, but pretty populated with lesbians, single and coupled, young and old, with and without children.

The summer I was finally pregnant, we had seats thirteen rows behind the home basket. To our three o'clock, behind the benches, was a lesbian couple with an infant daughter. They spent most of every game bottle-feeding her and changing her diaper, looking away from her only when someone cheered or booed. I spent a lot of time watching them, looking forward to our future (already knowing we'd be doing that times three).

To our nine o'clock sat Kelli and Rosie O'Donnell, a famously lesbian, famously pregnant couple. Both Kelli and I would waddle down and up to our seats, and for the first time since actually coming out, I felt part of a community I wanted to belong in. I was proud to be who I was, a stage that was many steps past acceptance.

It is well-documented that pregnancy brings out the nosiness in everyone else. Questions about my fertility, my pregnancy, my symptoms—nothing was out of bounds. I had worked hard to get pregnant and was happy to answer questions.

When they asked about my husband, though, an almost knee-jerk reaction to seeing a pregnant woman, I realized things were going to be different. Gender-neutral pronouns were not going to work. Once my kids were cognizant, I didn't want them to hear me using gender-neutral pronouns or avoiding conversations. If I was going to raise them to be strong and proud of who they were, I had to set the example. Having children was going to kick me so far out of the closet I would not be able to find the door back in.

I had nine months to practice. When strangers asked about "your husband," I corrected with "my partner." I was shocked by how easy it was. They quickly corrected themselves and moved on. Some, of course, took the opportunity to tell me how progressive they were by telling me that they already had a gay friend. Regardless, it was painless.

So during my nine months, I let everyone else worry about the complications of a triplet pregnancy and the possible stigma of having gay parents. I was serene; I just put my arms on my belly to feel those babies kick, and I knew, just knew, everything would be just fine.

"IT'S TOO BAD MAMI didn't come with us to this birthday party," Jacob said, looking out his window at the water treatment plant.

"Yes, she would have had fun," Anais said, looking out her side of the car at the canal alongside the highway, slowly bringing the Everglades' water to this urban sprawl.

"But I'm sure she's having lots of fun cleaning the house," I said, pulling off the turnpike and closing in on our destination. Palm trees were propped up by wooden stakes in the median.

"She could have met Julian. I'm going to marry him," Emma said, as our minivan pulled into the driveway. We could see the bounce house looming in the backyard.

Anais added, "She could have met Kaylee's parents. She has a dad and a brother. But only one mom."

13.

*Ben's Eyes**

⟹ LOUIE CREW ⟸

I loved Grandmama's. I loved the tin roof, the smell of the wood stove, the taste of the metal dipper, the tiny roof above the well, the tomatoes we picked and ate off the vine, the rope swing that hung on the tall hickory, but most of all Ben's eyes.

Long before six others and I integrated one of the high schools in Houston County, Georgia, in the early sixties, or before I became the drum major and broke the heart of the white football captain, back before I was a teenager and we lived on an Air Force Base in Texas, I used to spend two months of every summer at Grandmama's house in south Georgia.

My older sister, Hattie, who was thirteen then, teased me before everyone as her "country kid-brother." She went to Georgia with me the first time, but she didn't like the single-room house, the bed she had to share with Grandmama, the goats in the yard, the weeding and the hoeing, collard greens every day of the week, no radio, and the six-mile walk—one-way—to the movies. She stood it for about three weeks and then cried until Grandmama let her return early to "Texas civilization and the

---

*All the details in this story are true. The writer has fictionalized only the names of persons to respect their privacy.

twentieth century," as Hattie boasted to her girlfriends at our large playground on the base.

Ben was my older cousin, sixteen or seventeen, and he had gorgeous, round, bedroom eyes, with long lashes like the kind women pay to have made up false. Ben's face was a richer black than mine, with not even a hint of tan. He had generous cheeks and a lean chin. His strong red lips could not conceal the slight smile he kept as I stared at him for minutes at a time, not just when we rested in the shade to guzzle water from the Mason jar, but even while I rode with him on the rented single-seater, plowing Grandmama's field. I probably wasn't much help, but he made me feel that I was.

We watched for any rocks down the row. "Go get it, Cleveland," he would squeeze me, and I'd jump down, run ahead, and put it in the big drum, which we had hung on the back of the

---

LOUIE CREW is a native of Anniston, Alabama. He holds a master's from Auburn University, a PhD from the University of Alabama, and Episcopal seminary honorary doctorates. Ernest Clay is an international flight attendant. Ernest ("Cleveland" in the story) is a native of North Carolina but grew up as a "military brat" over much of the South. His family is rooted in Georgia, where he and Louie met and married. Louie is an emeritus English professor at Rutgers University. He has published four volumes of poetry: *Sunspots, Midnight Lessons, Lutibelle's Pew*, and *Queers! For Christ's Sake!*. The University of Michigan collects his papers.

Crew and Clay

tractor for our collection. At the end of the row, we would add these to the border, built up for more than fifty years around this field. Still the field continued to yield new chunks with each plowing.

"God makes them during the winter," Ben told me.

Ben had dropped out of school at fourteen, but anything he said convinced me, at least at the time that he said it. Most of the time he just sat silent, concentrating on the noisy tractor. Still short enough not to block his view, I braced myself on the narrow metal strip meant for his feet, and leaned against Ben's legs, just looking and looking and looking.

Ben was Grandmama's only help. Grandmama kept a picture of Ben's mama and daddy on the chifforobe near where she slept in the room. Ben's mama, my daddy's sister, a pleasantly fat woman with a broad, pretty face, sang the blues at backwoods clubs for black farmers all over south Georgia. His daddy, lean and less noticeable, more or less tagged along, or so I thought then from what Grandmama said whenever I asked about the picture.

"Fancy. Mighty fancy," my mother used to tell me about them, "but a bit dangerous, too." Ben's parents were killed in separate automobile wrecks, a week apart, when Ben was thirteen. Much later, when I was in high school and no longer going to the farm for summers, I would learn that Ben's daddy's accident had happened when the county police forced him off the road at high speed. They used the six cases of bonded whiskey in his trunk to prove that he was into "big crime."

Ben didn't talk about his people much, nor did he seem interested when Grandmama would answer my questions. While Grandmama and I cleaned up after supper, he usually sat over by the kerosene lamp looking at a *Jet* magazine, or studied his mustache with a pair of trimmers and a small hand mirror.

"You gonna break some gal's heart iffen you don't stop tryin' to be so pretty," Grandmama would tease him. "God done already give you sexy eyes. Why don't you leave well enough alone?"

Ben would laugh and continue to groom.

AFTER WE'D PUT AWAY everything, sometimes we lolled around on the porch, or we would swing. In the top of the old hickory, Ben had built a tree-house back when he had been my age, but I never got to see the inside. Long before I ever came to visit, Bessy Craddock, the girl who lived at the next house down the road, stepped on a weak limb, fell, and broke her arm. After that, Grandmama laid down the law: the hickory tree was only for swinging.

Sometimes I seem to conflate all those summer evenings into one, so much did I enjoy our times in that swing, but I remember one particular evening as distinct. It was sunset—dark reds and oranges—and then a streak of royal purple appeared just about as fast as Ben blinked his eyes. He sat on the seat and I sat in his lap, nose almost touching nose, my legs tight around his hips, my arms thrown loosely over his shoulders, his large hands clasping my ribs, as we swang higher and higher and higher. I did not grasp. I knew he held me.

Grandmama went to bed early, got up early. Sunrise. Sunset. That's what her "early" meant. "You young 'ens can do as you please, but if you want to live as long as I have, you'd better be payin attention. Leastaways, don't disturb my rest with no kerosene lamp. Those folks' pictures in *Jet* seem a bit highfalutin anyways . . ." She would natter on until she gave us the cue: "Now I'll get into my night clothes."

Ben and I would dutifully step outside. When we came back in, we'd make our way in the dark to our own side of the room. Even without a moon, starlight sufficed. Each of us had a special chair to hang our clothes on. I slipped into some short pajamas Mama had made for me, but, hot as Georgia stays at night in summer, Ben slept in his birthday suit.

Some nights, after we'd swung, Ben would not come to bed at once, but would go down the road to see Bessy and her brothers. One night a storm came up unexpectedly after he had left and I had gone to bed. It thundered and lightninged something terrible. Grandmama snored through it all, but I lay awake until well after midnight listening to the rain batter our tin roof and looking at the green hands on Grandmama's wind-up alarm clock, wondering whether Ben was dry. I awoke when I heard the tractor revving in the dark. He had stayed in the Craddocks' barn until the lightning stopped but had come back to put the tractor under the shed.

A few minutes later, the room deadly dark without even starlight, I felt cool air rush over me. He even sounded wet. I heard him sniffle as he closed the door. I heard him drip as he unlaced his shoes. I heard him peel off his socks. I heard a chair scrape the floor slightly as he tiptoed past it. I heard the zipper. I heard his buckle jiggle on the wooden floor. I heard him breathe and knew he must be arcing his T-shirt over his shoulders. It slapped the chair gently. I heard underwear ping his knees. Then silence. An interminable silence. Even under the covers I shivered knowing he stood there wet, exposed, although I could see only his blackness shadow the slightly lighter darkness of the room. I feared my eyes might glow in the dark like the hands on the clock, that he might know that I stared, so I slitted them. I held my breath to hear him breathing, slowly, evenly. A board squeaked slightly. I expected our bed to tilt to his weight, but still he stood there. It seemed an eternity.

When he did get in he moved to me at once, not after he

was asleep as he usually did. His wet chest sent goose-bumps down my back. His thick thighs seemed a bit drier at my hips. He sighed pleasantly through his nose as I warmed him. "Sleep well, my little heater; sleep well," he whispered softly.

I DIDN'T LOVE THE outhouse. That's about the only place where I ever envied Hattie and her *Texas civilization* during the entire summer. Hattie had made it worse by telling me even before we went to Georgia that first time together: "Snakes lay down there in the holes just waiting to bite any ass black enough and delicious enough to sit there, particularly if they decides to sit there too long. And the spiders. You just look up to the ceiling. They be waitin for you, country bumpkin!"

Mama had told me I should try not to use nasty public restrooms except for liquids and to plan my days so I'd be near home when I had to go. So the first time I went to Georgia, already warned by Hattie, I fixed my mind to see the outhouse as a public restroom. When I peeked at it and saw that it was a two-seater, that cinched it. Besides, the shack stood separate from Grandmama's house. How much more public could you get? I decided to wait all summer until I got back to Texas before I would go again, except for liquids.

By the third day, I must have looked mighty ashen. After supper Grandmama asked, "Boy, you feelin all right?"

"Yessum," I lied.

"You don't look it. Have you vomited or something?"

"Nome."

"Ben, you be out there with him all day on the tractor. Has this child seemed sick to you?"

"The boy probably just taking time to get used to eatin' real food," Ben said, lost in *Jet*.

"You regular?" Grandmama asked.

Hattie snickered. "Have you gone down with the creepy, crawly snakes every day?" she asked (she had not yet thrown her screaming fit to escape).

"Hush your mouth, girl, or I'll creepy, crawly you," Grandmama said to Hattie. Ben laughed like he was on my side. I bowed my head.

"Answer me, boy," Grandmama said gently.

She finally got out of me that I had been too scared to go. Grandmama wouldn't hear a word of it when I explained that Mama had told me never to use a public restroom.

"Ben, you go down there with him and don't either of you come back until he's done a job, you hear? Land's sake, all this Texas civilization will be the death of him for sure!"

I thought I could not do it with someone else there. At least the restroom at school had partitions for those that dared to use them. Here Ben's thigh touched mine and I nearly choked on the cigar which he lit, "to scare away everything," he said. "Take your time, Cleveland."

It began to get dark fast. We left the door open for the clean air, and looked far down the field where we'd plowed all day long.

"I didn't know that you is circumcised," Ben said.

"What?"

"I didn't know that you is circumcised," he repeated.

"What's that?"

He reached over and touched the head. "That," he said.

"What's 'circumcised'? Ain't you?"

"Nope. See."

He held his up into the twilight. "Pull back the skin like this," he said. "Your's been cut that way by the doctor soon as you born."

I looked at his, then at mine. "Is that why yours hard and mine soft?" I asked.

"Soft?" he asked. I had not noticed the hard knot mine had made.

"Why the doctors do that to me?" I asked.

"Beats me," he said. "Must have something to do with Texas civilization."

I did my job easily now.

"Don't be 'fraid, Cleveland. Just tell me when you want me here witchya. Besides, see this stick"—he leaned and reached just outside the door for an old broom handle he kept there— "you just take this pole and beat on the side before you ever come in here. That'll scare away anything that might harm you. Don't you listen to Hattie or everwho talks that way. Nobody can't make no sissie outa man like you."

I did not fear the outhouse anymore. Still I waited most times until I knew he was going so I could go at the same time.

I LIKED BEING WITH Ben even better outdoors on the tractor, leaning against his lap, or in the swing, or taking a break in the shade at the far end of the field, or having him snuggle up after he thought I'd gone to sleep. One night while he was still out, I took off my pajamas and hid them on the floor next to the wall under the bed, so Grandmama wouldn't see them and remember that I'd had them on. I wanted to feel Ben's smooth skin against mine.

And one day, right there on the tractor, I took mine out and studied it. "Why the doctors do that to me?"

"They didn't hurt it none. It's as good as mine," Ben said.

I felt him grow stiff. I turned and tried to straddle him like I did in the swing.

"Just a minute, child, lessen we kill ourselves on this here machine." He idled it at the end of the row. Far at the other end, clean white bedclothes whipped in the sun. In the shade

I looked long into Ben's eyes before and after I inspected un-circumcision.

BEFORE DADDY LEFT THE air force we got stationed back in Georgia, but when Grandmama fell sick one of my aunts moved in to take care of her cause Ben was away in the army and I was too busy with my paper route to laze away a summer in the country. By the time I took Home Ec in high school my sisters and brothers had gotten used to me and were plenty proud when I brought home a national prize for one of my recipes. Besides, I led the parade and had the captain of the football team sneaking over to see me four nights a week.

After I graduated, I took up modeling in the North. I heard that Ben had married—not Bessy Craddock, but a jazz singer named Eula Hines, from Macon. Mama said Eula was as much a looker as Ben's mama had been and that she and Ben lived just as dangerously as Ben's mama and daddy had.

So I had not seen Ben for about eighteen years when Grandmama died. I wanted to bring my lover with me to the funeral, but he decided it wouldn't be right to make our lives upstage theirs, especially at a time of grief. Anyways, Mama and Daddy had already met him and liked him a lot. I can't believe he would have surprised the others. But I didn't insist, since probably he would have been bored.

Neighbors and family came from all over.

They brought at least twenty kinds of deviled eggs, ten styles of fried chicken, and as many more of cornbread and collard greens, plus platter after platter of other good eatins. They laid it all out on long picnic tables in the pecan grove between the church and the cemetery. Eula's band played gospel music all day inside, before the sermon and the burial in the late afternoon. Since the church was too small to hold all of us at once, we went to and fro—from feast to the funeral in shifts.

About one o'clock, Ben himself arrived. He had filled out lots more, but was still muscle, not fat. I recognized him first by his eyes.

"She was a good woman, Cleveland; a good woman. It's a real loss to the world," he said, by way of greeting. All those outside came to greet him. Then Ben went in for some of the music. When he came out again, I eased to the same side of the food table so I could strike up a conversation with at least a touch of privacy.

I wanted to get off somewhere to ourselves, maybe alone in Grandmama's room, so I could tell him how much it meant to have learned about myself from someone who loved me, who was gentle, who taught me how to scare away the snakes. Before I met my lover, I discovered many people, both women and men, who didn't seem to know that you can also love the person you hold through the night.

I never had heard the word "gay" when Ben and I were together. When I hit puberty, I needed the word to describe myself, but I never thought Ben was. I still think he is not. But I knew that he had loved me when we did those things together.

"You remember the outhouse?" I asked.

"Cleveland, you were one scared little boy, yes indeed!" he said, and moved on down the table to get some ribs.

"You remember the night you came back from Bessy Craddock's all dripping wet?"

"No. I can't say as I do. Which time?"

"You remember the swing and the tractor?"

"What about 'em?"

"You don't remember?"

"Cleveland, you've grown up a fine young man. I always said you'd go farther than most of us. You may have begun scrawny, but like the turtle with the rabbit, you passed us all!"

"You really don't remember, do you?"

"Hey, little brother, what happened a long time ago is not important. Don't go troubling yourself." He forked a deviled egg, nibbled it, and lifted his chin to catch some yolk. "Man, it sure is good to see you!" He said it like he meant it. With his eyes, he indicated that perhaps we ought to mingle with the others.

I could not find a way to thank him.

14.

The Gathering

= JAMES VILLANUEVA =

Think of tamales boiling on a stove. The smell of *masa* turning into blankets for the pork meat inside, all wrapped in cornhusks the color of sunshine. This was the month of October and we weren't feeling November's chill just yet, but it was threatening with each day. Outside it was still warm enough for a light jacket, but when the sun set, cool air would roll over the plains and enter our house through every crack in the floors, walls, and ceiling. In spite of this, the smell of tamales found no escape. The corn smell seeped into the couch with bright flowers, into the maroon curtains with flower prints, the felt *Virgen de Guadalupe* portrait, the old yellow lounge chair bought at a garage sale, all of our clothes, and finally our very pores, becoming part of us.

At school the kids would say I smelled like a mixture of corn chips and bean dip. It wasn't, on the other hand, as bad as the time when my grandpa ran over a skunk on our way to church and when we entered the adobe building, which was considered holy grounds in the small town, all of the congregation turned and stared and whispered. Little old women with scarves covering their gray heads hunching over, reminding me of marigolds in the winter with barely enough strength to hold up to the lightest snow, all held handkerchiefs to their noses. Since that day, it wasn't so bad to be compared to bean dip. The smell of tamales is comforting if you've once smelled of skunk spray.

Seven of us lived in the old house. My *tío** and I lived in one bedroom on the far end of the house. There was a bathroom that connected us to my older *tío's* bedroom where we weren't allowed to go, but when he was gone we would always sneak in to listen to his eight-tracks. My little brother slept with my grandpa in a twin bed because he always had nightmares. The two slept in my grandma's room next to her queen-size bed and across from the altar that always had a candle, with a saint glued to the front, burning to chase away any bad spirits that haunted my little brother at night. My little brother and I had lived with our grandparents since birth because our mom had us at an early age and couldn't take care of us. When she dropped out of high school and moved away with a much older man, my brother and I became our grandparents' children.

On Sundays, the house was as loud as the *mariachi* bands my drunken *tíos* blared from their cars. Not even the loud bass from my *tío's* bedroom could mask the sound as Guns and Roses screamed *Sweet Child O' Mine* at a screeching pitch that hurt my seven-year-old ears. All of my *tías* would sit around the table with cornhusks in their palms, making sure to spread the *masa* evenly across the tamale hoods that keep the meat together. They made their own music as they gossiped and made tamales. Two *tías* would plop a spoonful of the dough onto the husk and smooth it out with a few strokes. Then they would pass it to two more *tías* who would stuff meat into the center and roll up the husk with the dough and meat inside. My grandma would tie them up with string and place them in a large pot to boil in the kitchen. It was a choreographed dance

---

*Tío is Spanish for uncle; *Tía* is Spanish for aunt.

and not a stroke was missed as they gossiped—*chisme* is what they called it—about neighbors, old *comadres* and anybody else who wasn't around.

Every Sunday in October the whole family gathered to make tamales in preparation for the upcoming holidays. All of my aunts and uncles would bring their children and we were forced to play with them because they were our *primos*. The tradition dated back to my great-grandparents who still did the same thing in a small village outside of Monterey, Mexico. My grandparents came from Austin, Texas, starting a new life on a chicken farm outside of Lubbock. They set up a small business selling chicken eggs to the neighbors and other people in the community. To make extra money, my grandpa worked as a farmhand for a cotton farmer. When I was older and told my grandma that I wanted to go to college so I wouldn't become a slave in the fields, her hand reached out across the space between us and her slap left a red mark on my cheek—a sting I can still feel today.

After a brief foray into the corporate world as a marketing director in Austin and then Chicago, JAMES VILLANUEVA has returned to his hometown of 7,000 people to write feature stories for *The Slatonite* in Slaton, Texas, where he is a staff writer and composition and circulation director. James is a contributing writer for *Latino Lubbock Magazine* and the *Lubbock-Avalanche Journal*. He has been featured in *Campus Pride, Texas Monthly Magazine,* and  *Southwest LGBT Press*. James is the author of the novel, *The Sweet Taste of Bread*, and has written various short stories for anthologies.

ON THIS PARTICULAR SUNDAY they gathered to plan our trip to Austin to visit a *tío* who was dying of a strange new disease. Nobody really knew much about it, but everyone had their theories about how he got it: "It was from prison; all those men grouped together, someone must have sneezed on him," my *tía*, the one who knew it all, would say. We all believed her because, well, no one else had any other explanations. From what everyone heard on the news and read in the papers, the other way he could have gotten it didn't make any sense because, well, because my *tío* was a man of Jesus.

In two weeks we would all take the cars and caravan eight hours south to Austin. The tamales we made on this day weren't for the holidays, but for the upcoming trip. Until then, they would make a home in the freezer. Playing off the energy of the adults, the children were wilder than usual. We ran and played in the house because if we went outside and ran around my grandma would get mad because we would catch a cough. Especially since *Tía* Christina's kids never zipped up their jackets. But after my cousin Junior fell off the bed and cried, sounding like an old barn owl hooting, the ban was lifted and my grandma *forced* us all outside where we could continue playing vampire and zombie in the rolling fields of harvested cotton.

The trip lasted a lifetime; at least when you've only been in the world for seven years it felt that way. We left at midnight in order to arrive in the early morning. It was the first time I had stayed up for an entire night. I watched Texas go by in the back seat of our station wagon filled with all kinds of blankets, pillows, snacks and stuffed animals for my little brother. The rolling plains soon made way for green fields and then rolling hills. When darkness gave way to light, the city of Austin awoke.

My relatives in Austin had a nice house to meet in. There

was a gate made out of bricks in the front yard that we would climb for hours. To me it was the biggest, most beautiful house I had ever seen. I was hesitant of venturing very far into the house because I was afraid a secret passageway would swallow me up and I would never be found.

The party was going to take all day to pull together and it was for *Tío* Jacob, who was dying from the weird disease that now had a name—AIDS. Everyone came out to greet us and give us hugs; there were a few tears because they were happy to see us. I was excited to have finally arrived. My imagination had us all falling off the planet. When we finally made our way inside some of my aunts stayed outside to help set up decorations for the big night that was still so far away. My *tío* Jacob sat on the couch inside. I was confused because he was a strong man and it didn't look like he was dying. My grandma told me to go hug him and so I did. Everyone hugged him, even my uncle Martin, who never hugged anyone.

MY COUSIN WHO LIVED there was ten days older than I, but a lifetime more mature and worldly. Danny knew more about the family and went to a better school, and so when we would color, his colorings were always detailed and inside the lines. Mine were always scattered and had purple cows with green spots, not nearly as impressive as the beautiful city skylines my cousin colored. I was always excited to hear new stories from Danny. He was always traveling to different states and claimed to have seen a mermaid the last time he was in California. I was jealous but didn't really know it, so I came up with the best stories I could. Only my stories involved riding oil rigs and catching rattlesnakes before they bit my four-year-old little brother.

It didn't take long before Danny took me by the arm and led

me outside to tell me about more of his adventures. This time he told me about going to the bar that his dad owned and meeting some famous person I had never heard of but I pretended to know who he was talking about anyways. We sat outside on the swing set and decided to have a flying competition. We would both swing as high as we could until the whole set rocked back and forth, then we jumped out of our seats and to see who could fly the furthest. Since he was taller he always won. Just when I was about to win, his mom saw me flying through the air from the kitchen window. She came running out screaming at us to stop and he was forced to stay in his room until lunch. This gave me the morning to roam freely on my own, but not until after I showered and got ready for the party. Even though the party wasn't until the evening, for some reason everyone was in a rush to get the festivities started.

I cleaned up and put on my favorite white button-up shirt. I sat on the porch, rocking back and forth on the porch swing, thinking about ways to explore the yard without getting too dirty. In a tent that was set up for the party by the garage, I could hear two men talking, both related to me in some way or another. At first they talked low about places to put the balloons and then there were angry words. "I don't understand why we have to throw him this big party, nobody told him to go out and do whatever it is he was doing all those years," the younger voice said.

"He is your cousin and you will respect him." It was his dad now, from what I figured out, who spoke back. He was slamming metal folding chairs around with so much force I thought he was going to break one.

"You said so yourself, you said that he was going to pay for what he was doing," the younger voice sounded like I do when I'm about to start crying.

"Either way, he's paying for it now and this may be the last birthday he has."

There was silence after that and nothing could be heard but the swing squeaking as I rocked quietly back and forth. It was all I could do to keep from crying because it was at that moment I knew, I knew even at that young age, it wasn't just *Tío* Jacob they were talking about, but someday it could just as easily be me. I heard a bird chirp, only it was a funny chirp, so I looked up into the trees and studied what appeared to be a mockingbird. I had always wanted to see a mockingbird and so my ears perked up to the bird in the tree that chirped away telling me her story.

THE MUSIC EVENTUALLY STARTED and we ate tons of food. There was *menudo*, sausage, potato salad, beans, and the tamales that we brought from Lubbock. For some reason they tasted different in Austin; they weren't as spicy as usual. My cousin ate four, but I could only eat three. A beer bottle was knocked over by some relative's clumsy feet and so the dancing began.

I have an uncle who wears funny boots every time he goes out dancing. They have half the heel chopped off. "Is better to dance with girls with," he said, with spit that smelled of beer flying towards my face. He, of course, was the first to dance and soon everyone joined in the festivities, hopping around like a chicken without its head. There were about thirty people on the dance floor and around forty standing, sitting or crouched on a wall. *Tío* Jacob sat in a corner alone, wearing a sweatshirt that had a longhorn on the front and giant letters that said TEXAS. Even though he sat alone at a table with tamale shells and half-eaten cake, he still smiled and looked at all of our crazy relatives. He wasn't sad being alone and he looked content for that brief moment. Then one of my *tías* motioned for him to join her on the dance floor, and he got up and was lost in the loud music and stomping boots of the dance floor.

If there was something I could do better than Danny, it was dancing. Danny, like other boys my age, thought dancing was dumb but I thought it was great. I was not like other boys. Even at seven years old I could keep up with *cumbas*. My grandma said I got it from my mom. "She was always the dancer in the family," she would say. So when everyone else was too drunk to notice, I joined the rest of the crowd, dancing until late into the night. Then, when I was so tired I couldn't dance anymore, I snuck away inside and fell asleep on my aunt's giant couch while the music went on outside without me.

Somewhere in the dark night, I woke to *Tío* Jacob's deep voice whispering loudly into a phone. He was talking to someone on the other end and at first I thought it was his girlfriend, but I didn't think he had a girlfriend. It was a guy named Josh. I remembered Josh, slightly; he was a friend of Jacob's from school. The two grew up together and had always been inseparable. I wondered for a moment why he wasn't at the party. Did he know Jacob was sick? I heard *Tío* Jacob tell Josh he loved him, which made me giggle a little because I had never heard two grown men speak like that. I stuffed my face into my pillow to muffle the small sounds of my giggles. It wasn't the type of laugh, however, that I made when I saw something funny on television or when a classmate made farting noises under his armpit, no, this was more like a sigh of nervous relief. I must have recognized something that night, realized that some of the feelings that had been slowly boiling inside me, my sense that I was different from other boys, maybe that difference was okay. I watched *Tío* Jacob hang up the phone, and as he walked, a dark figure in the dark room, he looked down at the brown carpet the entire time. He never noticed my presence. Seeing the way he walked made me sad, because it was the first time I noticed he was sad and he looked very tired. Then my exhaustion won out and moments after the door shut behind him, muffling the music from outside, I fell again into a deep sleep.

THE NEXT DAY WHILE the grown-ups cleaned up the mess from the previous night's celebration, *Tío* Jacob took Danny and me to the mall. It was the biggest mall I had ever seen and there were two levels. An escalator separated both floors and Danny and I could barely contain our excitement once we discovered the candy store. We were surrounded by candy and when a man came up to talk to *Tío* Jacob, Danny and I wandered off and lost our selves in the land of hard candies and bubble gum. Uncle Jacob gave each of us a plastic bag that looked like the bags used for vegetables at the grocery store, but here we could fill the bags with candy, any kind of candy we wanted. I headed straight towards the cherry sours. Danny, who suddenly did not seem nearly as excited as I was, watched the man talking to our uncle.

"That's the man," he said, holding his still empty bag while mine was becoming fuller by the second.

"What?"

"That's the man that made Jacob sick." Danny always called him Jacob, never *Tío* Jacob like I did.

"He got sneezed on, that's how he got sick."

"No, Jacob likes boys, he doesn't like girls. The way Jacob likes boys is wrong and that is why he is dying."

I looked at my uncle and he didn't look like he was threatened by this guy. He didn't look like this man wanted to kill him. I just assumed it was a conspiracy Danny had made up and so I ignored him and continued to fill my bag with candy. Danny became quiet and didn't even thank *Tío* Jacob for the candy. I thought that was rude, especially after the mean things he said about him, but I was too polite to say anything.

When we got home, Danny went to his room to eat his candy and I sat in the living room watching television and eating cherry sours. All the grown-ups were scattered around the house. This was the first and probably the last time during this trip I would be able to catch some of the cartoons I had been missing. Outside, even though it was November, it was bright and sunny. At home in Lubbock, there was already snow on the ground. I decided television was too boring when there was a beautiful day outside, inviting me to come out and play, so I twisted a bread tie around the top of my bag of candy, pretending it was a lock that only I knew the combination to. I set the candy on a table next to a giant lamp.

Outside, I saw *Tío* Jacob sitting on the swing set. I went over and sat next to him. We sat quietly. I never knew how to start conversations with grown-ups. I was just hoping he would start one with me. I looked up into the tree trying to find the mockingbird I was becoming acquainted with the evening before, but it was nowhere to be found.

"Who was that man?" I asked. "The one in the candy store?" It must have been all of the candy because suddenly I had a newfound valor.

"He's a very close friend of mine."

"What's his name?"

"Josh."

"Danny told me he made you sick, but that doesn't make sense." Then I told him to promise me he wouldn't tell Danny I told. He promised.

"Well," he looked up at the tree as if he knew about the mockingbird also. "I made myself sick. Sometimes people just get sick." He said nothing more. We sat on the swing and listened for our mutual friend, but we never heard its strange chirps.

"Are you scared?" I could feel tears starting to cloud my voice.

"No," he said. "You don't have to be, either."

"I am though," I said.

I was ashamed to be crying in front of him. Grandma told me not to be sad and not to cry when we were on our way to Austin. She said it would only make *Tío* Jacob feel worse.

To my surprise, he laughed. "You know," he said, "you can cry all you want. It's perfectly all right for you to feel sad." It was as though he had heard the conversation between Grandma and me.

"I don't want you to feel bad," I said, heaving, unsuccessfully trying to hold back more tears.

"I don't," he reached over and placed a warm hand on my shoulder. "I mean, yeah, I feel sad about leaving early," he said, casually, as if he were going on vacation. "I just know that I've had so much love in my life and I've had such a wonderful time that I am all right."

He got up from the swing and told me we should go inside to start getting ready for dinner. Then he ruffled my curly hair. I hated it when people ruffled my curly hair because it made it all puffy, but I let him anyways.

"You're just like your mom, never afraid to ask questions," he said as I wiped away the last of my tears. Then he looked at me with his dark brown eyes and I knew it was a compliment, not an insult. "You're gonna be all right, kid," he said as he walked inside. I followed behind.

WE LEFT AUSTIN EARLY the next morning and I slept the entire way back.

Two months later *Tío* Jacob died.

I wore my button-up white shirt to the funeral, the same

shirt I wore to his birthday party that now seemed so long ago. All the relatives that were dancing before now looked sad and tired. When the pallbearers went by, the teenager who complained about the party was helping carry the casket. I looked around the small funeral home at all the relatives who had greeted us with hugs when we arrived for the party; now everyone sat with their own families and wiped their eyes with tissues. I sat cuddled into my grandma's side the entire time. Danny sat with his mom, and to my surprise, he too was crying.

The funeral procession was long and slow. I looked out the window the entire time. It was a beautiful day. Once we got to the cemetery, everyone crowded around the burial plot. They had become familiar to me these past few weeks after all that time knowing them only from a distance. *Tío* Jacob's friends, who were still strangers to me, were there. There were even those who were close family friends, most out of respect, some out of curiosity, but also out of the gossip that came with the strange new disease. Danny stood next to his mom, fiddling with his jacket. Years later, when news of my coming out spread across the family conversations, Danny would become more and more of a stranger to me. At age eighteen, when I went away to college, I often thought about that scene around *Tío* Jacob's grave and wondered if it had been me in the casket, would I have been missed the same? At the time, though, all I could do was stand there in the cemetery, watching the charade. His casket was open and I could see his face from where I stood. I didn't want to stare so I fumbled with the buttons on my shirt instead. I stopped fumbling only long enough to look at my tío for the last time. He didn't look sick; he looked peaceful and serene. A light breeze fluttered some of the flowers. When the casket was closed, shutting him off from us until heaven, we all lined up with a fistful of dirt. My grandma told me that it was to put on the casket. When it came to my turn to put the dirt on the casket, I felt sad. I felt a knot in my throat and the tears starting to come, but I wiped them away and thought about sour cherries and felt comfort.

Grandma once told me heaven is the place where you get to meet up with everyone you ever loved in your life. The people there are happy and "you will know it's them by their hugs," she would say. I always imagined that *Tío* Jacob's hug would feel like dancing. It would feel like sunshine and I would feel as happy as a kid in a candy store, remembering every moment on earth but especially the sweet taste of cherry sours.

As we were driving away, I saw a man standing over *Tío* Jacob's casket. No other relatives were left; the only people there were from the funeral home. I looked closely to see if I could recognize the man. It was Josh.

AS THE YEARS WENT by and I grew older, my aunt's house in Austin became smaller and smaller. My oldest uncle moved out of our house in Lubbock, taking his eight-tracks with him, and then my other uncle left. My little brother finally learned to sleep alone and the house became empty except on Sundays when everyone would come over and eat tamales. Eventually, instead of spending spring breaks in Austin with my family, I was going to Colorado or New Mexico with my friends. The spring break of my junior year in high school, I went to Long-mont, Colorado, to go camping. One evening when we decided to take a break from the wilderness, a group of us took a trip to Fort Collins to catch the new *Scream* movie. While waiting in line, I looked over to see a nice young man with dirty blond hair and green eyes, glancing back. I soon learned he was a freshman at Colorado State, liked all of the *Scream* movies as well, and, yes, he too enjoyed sitting around campfires roasting marshmallows, which is where we spent the rest of the night. Sometime within the lost hours of night and under the Rocky Mountain stars, I had my first kiss with another man. Being in the arms of the young man whose name now escapes me, I knew I was living the life *Tío* Jacob talked about. The kind of life where, no matter how bad things got, I would still have someone to love and who would love me. Even though it was my first kiss, it wasn't the first time I knew I was gay; no, there were many firsts. The first time I danced in the Austin humidity in celebration of a life cut short. The first time I let the darkness of my aunt's living room comfort me while listening in on *Tío* Jacob's conversation with his lover. The first time I saw the kind of love *Tío* Jacob had for Josh. All were first glimpses into a future I once feared. In the Rocky Mountains, far away from all that was familiar, I knew I was all right. The young man and I promised to meet up that summer, and although we never did, I went back to Texas, dreaming the whole way back about my next escape.

Uncle Jacob's name eventually disappeared from everyone's lips and then one day he was gone from our minds altogether.

Danny joined the military and I went away to college.

Some time during those years, AIDS became less obscure. Born in 1981 and the first generation to never know a world without AIDS, we were warned every day of our lives of its dangers. Of course, it was no longer a gay cancer; it was now everyone's fear. Coming out to my family, whose only experience with homosexuals was whispers and stares, the glaring self-righteousness of blame, even as family love held true, was a challenge. But, I found in myself the need to live. So that's what I did. I lived my life as best I could because in the back of my mind I often wondered if I would live to see the age of thirty. I couldn't help it. It's what I was taught. Some time in my early twenties, I came to the realization that death has nothing to do with living; they are two separate entities each as different as night and day. To live fully one cannot constantly exist under the heavy hand of death. Love, however, in all its colors, can and most often will fill those voids created by whispers, stares, suspicions, and rumors that can sometimes silence people's lives and even follow them into death.

While in college I would come home for the holidays to the worn-out furniture, to my aging grandmother, and to the familiar smell of corn husks with the sound of *chismes* as my aunts worked their choreographed dance of the tamales. During one break I brought home someone I loved. He was a young man who came from a small town like me, whose Sunday afternoons also were filled with Mariachi music and Sunday dinners. Everyone welcomed him. The sight of my *tías* hugging him and my *tíos* chatting with him made me remember *Tío* Jacob. "You're gonna be all right kid," his soft voice hovered in the air before drifting away into an unknown mist where there is always music playing, people dancing, mockingbirds singing, and we are all greeted with the warm hugs of remembered friends.

15.

When Heaven and Hell Meet

⇒ VICKIE L. SPRAY ⇐

for Ingrid

I tried to save her for Jesus and then I slept with her. It wasn't her fault. Her nonchalance concerning the book by Pat Boone I gave her on how to be free from homosexuality, the fact that at twenty she was a worldly three years older than me, and the absolute draw-in—she knew how to fix cars—all overrode my commitment to heterosexuality and, for a short while, to Jesus. She worked at the hospital and would come into the diner where I worked as a waitress. The place was actually one of those leftover American structures with an ice cream fountain within a pharmacy on the corner of a mostly deserted downtown. It was All-American but with a Southern twist. You could get grits by the bowl and cornbread with your chili. We served breakfast in the morning and hamburgers and a dinner special in between orders for banana splits, root beer floats, and sundaes in the afternoon.

In the way that Southern small towns create personas around people via the grapevine of hearsay, I had learned she might be one of *those* people. My sources were friends who were mildly curious, others who were very curious, and a peripheral mutual acquaintance who had found herself at a party once with friends of a friend who knew some people who knew some of *those* people. The timing of all this dependable information reaching me, if not for the subject matter, could have been divinely inspired. All my years of having a crush on my gym teacher, my preference for being within the realm of female energy and my night visions of women's lips, women's hair, and women's touch became concentrated on the woman who sat in my booth as I leaned in for her order.

There was more to it than that. She lived with a woman at the time. I had no doubt, given my inside scoop into her life, that they were living as a couple. This was such a blatant rule breaker that I wondered how she could possibly look so normal, simply sitting here ordering her lunch, given her overt life of degradation. The incongruence of her way of life and the normalcy of her appearance snapped in my mind each day as she gave her order for a hamburger, extra mayo, and sweet tea, no lemon. She ate like a normal person. She paid her bill like a normal person and left a tip like a normal person.

VICKIE L. SPRAY is a spiritual counselor with a practice in Tallahassee, Florida. Writing saved her from despair and created, among other works, a novel titled Rose Painted Waters, about a young girl who wants to become a mermaid at a Florida tourist attraction as a way of deliverance from her family of origin. Her passion  is assisting people who want to transform their world by healing the wounds of childhood, religion and culture. She lives with her partner on six acres near a river where the manatee swim and swallowtail kites fly.

Sahra Hunes

Due to having been born into a crazy family, I was, at seventeen, living on my own in a two-room apartment. I would go home after work and churn with the strange possibility of a woman living the life of a lesbian. My experience with males thus far had lacked any real significance. Whenever I found myself within the realm of romantic possibility, I always felt I was in one bubble and he was in another. There wasn't anything wrong with his bubble. It was just that we would never be able to remove the thin layer of our differences and I found that intolerable. But did that mean I was a lesbian? The word itself was, in 1975, one of the most degrading words a woman could be called. A lesbian was the antithesis of what a woman should be, was meant to be, and—the most damning—who God created her to be. Lesbians were too ugly to get a man, could not be trusted around children, and hated all men.

I was a girl living in a small Southern town where the lines between what should be and what should not be were clearly demarcated for everyone from age two and up. Women did not live together as a couple in this world. Women loved men. Women got married to men and went shopping with their girlfriends. Women had babies and then they had grandchildren. Then they took care of her parents and then they took care of his parents and then they died and the pastor would say how giving and loving they had always been. I was wise enough to see that women lived within a tight tube of self-sacrifice, and I was desperate enough to imagine myself falling into the reproachful world of love between two women.

I did not have a place in my brain for non-familial relationships between women outside the realm of church circles, kitchenware parties, and friends partying with boys in the woods on Saturday nights. My mind constantly lingered on what the lives of two women in *that* kind of relationship must be like.

Who did the dishes if they were both women? Who took out the trash? I pictured them beside each other in a shared bed of abomination. Which one played the part of the man? And, yes, like the gerbil on its wheel in a closed cage of captivity, my mind played over and over the *how* of their sex lives. This woman who showed up at five minutes after twelve almost every day was walking within a world way outside the boundaries of acceptable as I scurried along the edges of temptation.

I PRAYED. IT DID not help. I went to church and looked at the women who had short hair and short fingernails. I do not remember actually ever hearing it, but somewhere in my cultural upbringing I had gleaned that women who had lesbian inclinations had short hair and short fingernails. I gravitated toward these women. I always seemed to sit next to them and sought them out for answers to my questions about religion and God. I assuaged my guilt by not nesting within their church hugs of hello and farewell.

One woman at Wednesday services seemed to take a particular liking to me. She was the one who gave me the Pat Boone book to give to my "friend who was immersed in women's sexual affections." I had blurted out one night at women's group that I might possibly know a woman who was trapped within the world of homosexuality. The next week, after group, the woman had walked me to my oxidized-burgundy Volkswagen hatchback. I could tell she was nervous but she seemed intent on walking beside me as if we were sharing an evening stroll in the night air. Before we reached the end of the church parking where I habitually parked, we accidentally touched shoulders and she jolted away and nearly stopped as if to turn around and run back through the church doors for safety. She smiled apologetically, as though she had tripped, and regained her resolve to carry on courageously toward her self-appointed task. She turned to me as we reached the light post next to my car, the light shining amber against the side of her face. A shadow of gray split her face as she smiled and handed me the book.

"It's never too late to rid yourself of those kinds of desires," she said.

I shuddered at the possibility that she might know my recent thoughts on the subject of women loving women. Then I suddenly saw her in a different light. Behind the outer layer of Southern politeness, there was a hardness, as if she had steeled herself against something many years ago and had remained alert for possible encroachments on her resolve. Over the next few years of my young life, I would recognize this look in women's eyes over and over again.

I read the book. It served two purposes. The first was to let me know there were evidently *lots* of people outside of my small-town, narrow-street experience who had strong feelings toward the same sex. Of course, everyone in the book had done battle against their homosexuality and *won*! Still, they had at one time lusted after someone of their own gender. This provoked a deep desire in me to meet these people. The second purpose was that when the object of my intrigue blithely brought the book back to me and said in the most nonjudgmental way a heathen could that the book was not for her, I was introduced to the novel notion that the leaders of my church might not have all the right answers for everybody, which was shocking to my religion-soaked brain.

It wasn't long before I found myself flirting with her when she came in for lunch. Of course, I had no idea if I was doing it right. How is a woman supposed to flirt with a woman? Is it the same as flirting with a man? She ignored me. It seems silly to say it now, but I had forgotten she had a girlfriend. Well, I had not forgotten exactly. I had yet to learn what rules applied to the lesbian world and how those rules compared to my known world of heterosexuality. Movies, my own parents, my friends' parents, the entire world, it seemed, had taught me how heterosexuals behave with one another, but I was clueless to the laws governing romantic relationships between women. If two women were together, did that mean the same thing as when a male and female were together in that they were "spoken for" and out of the game of playing with others?

I admit that even after she ignored me, and even after realizing that indeed some of the same rules applied in this new world, my curiosity, lust and mind-frenzy prevented me from comprehending where my desire ended and their relationship began. I did not have a proper respect for their relationship and I found myself at her booth and in her face as often as my obligations to my other patrons would allow.

WHILE ALL THIS INTERNAL drama was occurring, I heard from a friend that a friend of a friend had segued into a circle of women who were older and settled in the world of women loving women. She was brought into this circle by a woman she had met bowling. My friend said that she would not call these events "dates," but she was rumored to have exclaimed one night after a number of drinks that she might *at least* be bisexual.

I had not known there was a third choice! For a few weeks I was ecstatic. Maybe I did not have to go *all the way* into this strange land of Lesbos. Maybe I did not have to risk my identity as a woman who was a spiritual seeker, my place as an accepted member of society! I could be a bisexual! What a relief! This relief was short lived, however. Though bisexuality could offer a gray area, which seemed a more acceptable stance in the eyes of God and the men who made up all these rules,

I had to be honest; even if I were bisexual, I was developing a preference for women. I knew I was going to have to go deep into this jungle of sin to satisfy my newly discovered passion.

Then I heard about *the bar*. The woman who had infiltrated (my word, not hers) the circle of lesbian friends shared her newfound information with gusto, bordering (I thought) on treason. I stood as still and quiet as a sponge as she swaggered about in her position of "at least bisexual" and explained to the rest of us that there was a bar where these women go to party. It was called The Cactus and it was about an hour away from my two-room apartment.

The furor that had been building from my hours of sitting on church pews near God-loving women whose sweet perfume drifted around me, from the lunch-rush rebuff that my flirtations brought upon me, and now the talk of *real* lesbians sitting around, leisurely and secure, like husband and wife, exploded into a Friday night plan. I was going to The Cactus.

I knew I would need two things to go through with this. I would need to dress as manly as I could and I would need a bottle of wine. I knew (from the same place I knew everything else about this underground world of women) that a lesbian could be like a man or like a woman. Because I played softball, had always been tomboyish, and was a little envious of the rights of men, I chose the side that had the best chance of accomplishing the feat of meeting another woman like myself. I wore hiking boots and an oversized sweater. My hair was fairly short, though I wished I had thought to get it cut. The wine was a necessity because (as I had also learned from the rumor mill) if you walked into a place like that unaccompanied you could fully expect to be sexually accosted by women waiting for just such a chance. I was okay with that. Drinking the wine beforehand would make sure I stayed that way.

There was, however, something I forgot until I was well on my way into that cheap bottle of wine. I was underage. It is true that desperate minds will mother inventions. As I drove, enveloped within the ping-ping sound of my VW, I invented a lie. By the time I reached the parking lot that had been described to me, I had what I thought was a decent enough story to get me into The Cactus.

I finished the bottle as I sat and watched people come and go. Again, I was astounded at how *normal* everyone looked. Well, not everyone. I did think that a few of the women were men until I got a side view and detected breasts or overheard some girlish laughter. And I mistook a small-bodied man for a woman until I heard him say something to the man next to him as they walked in front of my car on the way to the bar's entrance. What I did not see, which I think I had expected, was shame. I didn't know beforehand that I had this expectation. Of course, we project what we are feeling ourselves, and so their carefree jaunts across the parking lot took me by surprise. They seemed so carefree and blatant about where they were going! Of course, even with the wine, thoughts of a religious explanation for their lack of shame intruded on my excited and confused state of mind. I thought these people were probably so far into their sin that they were indeed the "abomination" my pastor spoke of several Sundays ago—having lived in sin for so long, they had lost all semblance of a godly conscience.

This was a sobering thought. I suddenly realized that if I went any further, I might risk taking myself beyond the reach of God. If I acted on this Friday night venture, I might step irrevocably beyond any chance at the life of marriage, children, and acceptability for which I was destined many years ago in the meeting of my father's sperm and my mother's waiting egg.

I got out of my car.

Two MEN SAT ON short stools by the door. Both had mustaches, which relieved me of the need for a time-consuming gender analysis. Then it occurred to me that having two men at the door would be beneficial, possibly increasing the chances that my lie would gain my entrance into the bar. From where I stood, I could see that smoke hung within the dim reach of a few lights scattered around a room full of loud music and raucous conversation. Screams of laughter burst amidst the sporadic crack of balls on a pool table. Both men looked at me with the kind of interest I would expect from bouncers on duty.

"Hey, guys," I said, trying to appear nonchalant.

Both had large flashlights for the purpose of checking identification. I handed them the picture of a Georgia boy I had dated a few times. Georgia boy and I had ended up in his father's barn the last time I saw him. He had mailed me this picture after I stopped writing and now I was using it as a way to get into a gay bar.

"I'm trying to find my friend. He said he would be here tonight. Have you seen him yet?"

They both lifted flashlights to the picture and saw a boy of maybe eighteen, with delicate features and a sly smile.

"No, don't think so," the one on the left said. The other shook his head and looked toward the bar, no longer interested in the conversation.

"OK, I'll wait for him then. How much?" I said, as I pulled out my men's wallet from my back pocket.

"Four," he said as he handed the picture back to me.

And that was it. I was in! I walked without hesitation directly to the bar without looking left or right. The bartender nodded in my direction, "Whatcha have, butch?"

He called me butch!

I ordered a beer as offhandedly as I could manage, given the excitement of my victory, and looked around for the women I knew would be headed my way very soon. A woman in a long sequined dress was singing a Diana Ross song. I had just had the thought that she sounded so much like Diana Ross that she could *be* Diana Ross when I realized she was actually a man *dressed* like Diana Ross. My know-it-all "at least bisexual" acquaintance had not told me of such things and I was trying not to appear stunned. The bartender grabbed my money, made change, and threw it in his tip jar.

I detected what I thought were women huddled around the small stage. I watched a man dressed in chaps come from a dark corner of the bar and put a dollar bill in the top of what I now know was a drag queen's nylons.

I slugged down my beer and ordered another. It appeared I was going to have to wait until after the show before the women started trying to get me into their sexual grasp. After my third beer, and after the last drag queen, this time a Bette Midler impersonator, left the stage, I poised myself for the onslaught. None came. I was as invisible as a fly sitting on a fly swatter.

My mind reeled with possible explanations. There were women here who were not attached to anyone. Why had they not come over? I wasn't the cutest thing in the world but I certainly was as cute as some of the women whose arms were wrapped around other women's shoulders.

Maybe that was it!? Maybe I was supposed to be the pursuer! I was dressed as the man, after all. The very idea deflated me, so I ordered another beer. And then another. I slipped into a dazed depression as I realized I was way beyond my social capabilities. This foreign land of gender-bending, and who says what to whom, and who does what to whom, and who takes out the trash and who does the dishes were beyond me and what was I doing trying to step into this unknown area of human nature anyway?

I did end up having a conversation with a boy about my age (had *he* used a picture of an old boyfriend to get in?) who promised to introduce me to his aunt if I came back next week. I left too drunk to drive and too depressed to care.

AS FATE WOULD HAVE it, the next week, my favorite lesbian patron began to return some of my clumsy flirtations with some expert statements and cautious flirtations of her own. It seems she and her lover had reached a rough spot. She handled this bump in the road the way a lot of young people, both homosexual and heterosexual, do when relationships begin to slip toward the miserable: she began to look for comfort elsewhere.

For a moment, I panicked. So here I was after months of questions, questions and more questions, about to get some answers, answers, answers. From a *real* lesbian who no doubt knew exactly who does what to whom.

"What are you doing after work?" she asked me as I put her hamburger, extra mayo, and sweet tea, no lemon on the table in front of her breasts. It was a Wednesday. Church night.

"Just going home."

"No church?"

She smiled hesitantly and I interpreted that as respect for my religious confusion and her willingness to totally back off if I wanted her to. I did not want her to.

"Not tonight," I said.

Oh, the glory of first love!

I learned that the new path of first love is strewn with soul-glitter. Newness. It was all new. I had not seen this kind of love on television. The few stories I had read in pulp fiction novels did not mirror two young women driving on hot Southern nights through a small Southern town singing Donna Summer songs and kissing beneath the shelter of the live oak tree. I fell into her as though I had known her all my life. Whatever the world, the churches, the rules said about two women loving each other did not apply to us because they did not make any sense compared to this delight, this feeling of rightness. There was nothing more right than loving her.

THE YOUTH YEARS OF a girl coming out and falling in love in a small Southern town are full of glistening tales but also of dark lessons of people's ignorance and fear. She has to, or *feels* that she has to, explain herself. She's young and does not yet understand that explanations of how two women love each other are nobody's business, that she does not need anyone's permission. The internalized homophobia will rear its subtle influence for years to come until she finds her own resolve.

And then there is the whole God thing. How does a young woman who is a spiritual seeker and also a lesbian reconcile her relationship to God? It seemed like the first thing that needed to happen was for me to toss out everything I had been told that did not feel right to my spirit. I had to be honest and real and unflinching because I needed to be sure that if I were going to give up God, it had to be because I was certain that God and my gender preference could not live harmoniously within me.

It is a private journey, this reconciling yourself with the spiritual. All the voices of religion and other people's opinions about who God is and how the divine does or does not influence the happenings of our earthly plane must be sorted through. The fear of retribution and being kicked down the street if you step out of line must be put aside while the spirit within instructs on what is real and what is of man. Working within the heavy cloud of Southern culture made my personal journey particularly cumbersome. I was continuously burdened by daily reminders of how loving a woman was wrong, of how wrong I was, of how I had become an "abomination to God."

I quit going to church.

In my mind, giving up church was synonymous with giving up God. Of course, it wasn't long before I discovered this was untrue. The Divine has a way of sticking around even when a young lesbian feels like she must forgo all things divine in her attempt to discover *her* truth. I was one of the fortunate ones. Coming out to myself, falling in love for the first time, reconciling the spiritual with the accepted rules of religion, coming out to co-workers, friends and family and the watchful eyes of a small town felt perilous and was frightening. I witnessed several women scurry back into the safe harbor of the heterosexual world. I made my own fatalistic segues back into the "normal" world of relationships with men until I finally gave in and surrendered to my true nature.

What a relief. And now I am left with the memories of me, as a young woman, breathing the humid air of her upbringing, making the first steps toward claiming herself, her God and her life, and being very happy with how it all worked out.

16.

Calling

O when may it suffice?
That is Heaven's part, our part
To murmur name upon name. . . .
                    — WILLIAM BUTLER YEATS

⇒ ED MADDEN ⇐

S oon after I came out, I began telling my friends a story. It was a story I found myself repeating, as if it could begin to mean what I wanted it to mean only through repetition. It is a bit like saying, "I love you," which I say over and over hoping that if I say it often enough the words will begin to mean something. That is, I suppose, the nature of repetition and of remembrance. The story is about the rural community in Arkansas where I grew up. It is about going home, and it is about not being able to go home. It is a story about being gay.

Three years before I came out to my family my mother called to tell me about the death of Paul. It appeared to be simply another story in the litany of hometown events she recounted as she filled me in on the local news during our telephone conversations. Paul was about eight years older than I and we had gone to the same Beedeville Church of Christ. He joined the Navy right after high school, and I can remember his coming to church, an officious and beaming figure of manhood and respectability, in dress whites and military crew cut. A few years after that, he seemed to disappear from the local conversation. I had, in fact, forgotten about Paul until my mother told me he had died. At some point, between his proud homecomings as a military man and my mother's recollections on the telephone, Paul had come out of the closet, dropped out of the Navy, and moved to Austin, Texas. No one talked about him at home. His father had disowned him. He had moved even farther away—to San Francisco. And then he had contracted AIDS. During the summer of 1991, his brother and sister drove to California and brought him home, where he died a couple of days later. The funeral service was in his parents' house, and only the family was invited, my mother noted.

Was my mother speaking indirectly to me? Surely she must have had her suspicions by then. This story—confirming how shameful it was to have a gay son—only strengthened my fears about coming out to my own family. I don't know whether Paul and his father ever reconciled. I don't know how, or if, the community mourned his death. All I know is that a gay man returned home and died, and no one was invited to remember him.

When my mother related this story to me, I had been to only six funerals in my life, those of Ashley, a high school friend; Ed, my cousin's fiancé; two grandparents; an aunt; and, only months before my mother's call, an Austin man who had died of AIDS.

Ashley had died in an airplane accident a few years after we graduated—a daring Icarus flying a small plane (probably a crop-duster) too low; the wheels catching the utility wires that crisscross the farms of Jackson County. Like all funerals, his was a community ritual; for those of us who were fledgling adults, it was a naming of our common mortality and our common home, even as we were letting go of our hometown and finding other communities.

My cousin Tara's fiancé died mere months before their wedding. Coming home from working on their house one night, Ed fell asleep at the wheel. I remember most that Tara refused to call me by my name, which was also his name, and I remember her screams at the cemetery, her distress because she couldn't see him (it was a closed casket funeral, because of the accident). We each buried our own private images of him. I fumbled with a name.

When I entered graduate school, I had changed my name. I became "Ed," not "Eddie." It is in the nature of growing up; we

Forrest Clonts

Born on a rice and soybean farm in Arkansas, ED MADDEN is an associate professor of English and director of women's and gender studies at the University of South Carolina. He is the author of four books of poetry: *Signals*, which won the South Carolina Poetry Book Award; *Prodigal: Variations*; and *Nest*. He is the author of *Tiresian Poetics*, a study of sexuality in early twentieth-century literature, and co-editor of *Irish Studies: Geographies and Genders*, as well as *Out Loud: The Best of Rainbow Radio*. In 2006, he won the Legacy Award from the Human Rights Campaign of the Carolinas for a history of public advocacy on behalf of LGBT people. He lives in Columbia, South Carolina, with his husband, Bert, partner in life, gardening, and activism.

try to lose the diminutives, the nicknames, the identities we could not choose for ourselves. Names are not easy, particularly the name "homosexual." It took me more than twenty years to name myself a homosexual, and it was not a name I accepted easily or willingly. To do so is to call myself an outsider, a deviant, queer. There does not seem to be room for queers in a small Southern town, on the family farm, in the fundamentalist church, among the honeysuckle and dewberries and soybean fields of rural Arkansas, all places I called home. I am both inside and outside: the imposter in the taxonomies—all those fine names for difference. Being gay is the wild card, the anomaly; it is the unknown factor, its origins and explanations far too numerous and obscure—the little farm boy who wrote poetry. How can I explain it? How can I not try?

THE COMING OUT STORY has its common features, no matter how many times it is told: the sense of difference, the feeling of being an outsider no matter how much a part of a community you are. "How long have you known?" we are asked. Always, and yet never. I have known and not known for so long, it is hard to tell where remembrance ends and repression begins. Like winter wheat, the green in the midst of fields of gray, the seasons and meanings blur in the life of the tale itself, the tale of a life. Only when I finally had a name for it, and gave myself that name, did I know. And then nothing was changed, and everything.

Now it seems a way of knowing, a way of seeing and reseeing. I am taking a friend home, and I see everything through his eyes. I see the long dirt roads. I trace the family histories in the portraits hanging in the hallway. I am hugging my father and mother. I am at my brother's wedding, singing. I am tracing the roots of the mulberry tree in the front yard, its seedlings sprouting all around the house. I am no longer at ease here. No longer at home.

There is a consolation in knowing from a distance, both literal and figurative, nostalgia on the horizon like an unfamiliar scar. And yet there is a certain pleasure to be had in the act of confession, like grace, the smell of wet earth under a green February sky. The consolation of distance and the intimacy of confession meet in the act of remembering, in the act of telling our stories. The theologian Fredrick Buechner has written of our need "to enter that still room within us all where the past lives on as part of the present, where the dead are alive again, where we are most alive ourselves to the long journeys of our lives with all their twistings and turnings and to where our journeys have brought us." There is a room called remember, its windows each a narrative, its anteroom regret. We enter the room in the past tense, we exit in either the present or the conditional: what we remember, the reasons why, the way things might have been.

JUNE 5, 1987. REDWING blackbirds shout themselves hoarse from the oaks of the cemetery. A crop-duster drones above a nearby rice field. The long caravan of cars that left the church is still arriving, the dust drifting in waves that coat the dull green rows of grain sorghum and soybeans, dust still hanging in air hot with the smell of Arkansas honeysuckle and vetch and the sweet maroon ferment of funeral roses. I breathe deeply: the summer grass is at the verge of brown, freshly mown, the musty, almost acrid earth of this sandy hillside, piled by the grave. These things must be remembered, like the daffodils that marked my grandma's death, standing in bright and silent clusters of mourning at the cemetery, dotting her yard like relatives, nodding, touching, cousins laughing, flaring their bright lives against the gray spring wind.

Grandpa's flowers are scattered down the line of tombstones, decorating the graves of his wife, his children; it seems the office of aunts to gather the blooms, to drape these odd dots and splashes against brown earth, gray stone. We the men, the sons and grandsons, take the shovels in groups of three, marking our ties with the thuds that fill the grave: it is love, it is something of God. And there must be a word to fill the hole it creates.

When my Aunt Etta was dying, she chose the hymns for her funeral, and I think she chose the short inspirational verse that appeared in the program at the funeral service. I do not now remember that poem. What I do remember is the graveside service. Uncle Henry had planned ahead, brought shovels to the cemetery in his pickup so that we could bury her ourselves, an act that seemed both personal and final. What was not planned was the watermelon. It was hot, a July afternoon, and Uncle Henry sent my brother and me to the farm shop, just down the road, to get a watermelon that was chilling in the freezer there, along with an ice chest full of Cokes. We returned, our arms full of grace—the chunks of pink sugar, the sweet juice, wet seeds and rinds like green jewels on the cemetery lawn, our mouths full of fruit and affirmation.

For me, the act of remembrance is inextricable from the funeral. In Jackson County, Arkansas, my home, in places like Cowlake, Hickory Ridge, and Beedeville, the service is almost always in a church, rarely a funeral home, and the community acts as a community, showing up for visitations at the funeral home, turning out for both church and graveside services, making food for the family. I think that is what disturbed me about Paul's funeral in his parents' home—the community was not invited to be a community. Nor was the man affirmed as part of that community. The gay man's death was a marker, a naming of rupture, of dysfunction.

WHEN I WENT TO an AIDS funeral in Austin with a friend, there were three visible communities: the dead man's friends from the magazine staff on which he worked, his gay friends, and his family. Except for the man's lover and his nurse-caseworker, who mingled freely, the three groups did not mix. Their only communion was the act of remembrance, of standing up before the group and telling stories about Norbert.

Norbert's sister had written a poem, which was read by someone else, since she was emotionally unable to. Like much funeral poetry, like all those memorial tributes in the daily newspaper, it was aesthetically forgettable. But it was nonetheless powerful, even when the reader lapsed into a singsong reading and the meter slipped awkwardly into unaccented gallops, even when the individual and personal was spoken through cliché. That, after all, is the nature of language: the inevitability of the cliché, the used. It is why we must say, "I love you," over and over again, repeating it with dumb fingers, mute skin.

In Mark Twain's *Huckleberry Finn*, the young poet, Emmeline Grangerford, kept a scrapbook of obituaries and accidents, and before her own death at age fifteen she became known for her funeral poetry, her tributes to the dead. She is, of course, a character both pathetic and parodic, and one knows from the one example in the novel that her elegies were indescribably bad, though Huck assures us, "It was very good poetry." I cannot help but think that even though Twain is obviously poking fun at her, as well as at any sentimental or clichéd art, we may recognize in Emmeline Grangerford the impossible possibilities of language. Everyone dies: that is a statement both tragic and banal. But the name of that death is important; we write it in stone. Poems and obituaries, like tombstone rubbings, repeat the name, recall the life. We remember.

My grandpa's little brother, Oscar, died when he was about eight years old. I know little about him, though I do have a couple of his elementary school textbooks and his copy of *Pilgrim's Progress* (subtitled "In One Syllable Words for Young People"). After Aunt Etta died, my parents and I were going through some of my deceased grandparents belongings, which had been stored away by another aunt, and we found a box of photos and memorabilia from my great-grandmother. There were photos, mostly of people we did not know, though we did recognize family resemblances—invisible ancestors, the pictures unlabeled, faces unnamed. We also found a prayer cloth, a square of moth-eaten green felt, embroidered with harps and swirls and arcane symbols.

My dad explained that Oscar's grandmother, my great-great-grandmother, was a member of a Southern evangelical church called the Church of the Brethren. The cloth had probably been prayed over by a faith healer within the church, or perhaps one of the "tinkers" who came through each year with their tools and their charms. It was kept in Oscar's sickroom, a fetish, or a quilt perhaps. My great-grandmother, a member of another church, hadn't liked the cloth, but had allowed it in his room, although probably not on his bed. Strangely, though, she kept it. Its symbols are now impenetrable, a code both intensely personal and part of a greater religious language. Other than a few books, it is the only reminder of Oscar: a piece of cloth, a text stitched with history and disease and hope.

As we were sorting through photos and newspapers, my mom also came across a small leather journal. For the most part it was the account book of a distant Irish ancestor, a handyman who shoed horses, forged clappers for bells, and built coffins.

But it had been recycled, for in the margins were the notes and poems of a little boy. Near the end of the book, after the short love poems to several little girlfriends, after the repeated refrain, "Flowers may fade, Leaves may die, True friends may forget you, But never will I," there was the final signature, "Scribbled by John Jay Madden." My great-grandfather was also a farm boy who wrote poetry.

WHEN I WAS BAPTIZED at the age of eight, I was told that I was to become a new man. It is what we are taught. At baptism, the old man of sin dies and a new man comes up from the grave, like Jesus. We are buried in water and raised in the language of a new life. The language is still familiar to me, even though the occasion is now so distant. I wonder what I was thinking then, during that gospel meeting, a revival at my home church. I know that I was terrified of hell. I know that I was just discovering my sexuality, which I'm sure had a great deal to do with my consciousness of sin. I remember walking up the aisle during the invitation song—I can still recall how I felt—and I still feel in my dreams, sometimes, that sense of being someone else, of watching myself, the singing all around me, the heat, the fear of hell.

The song was one of those many hymns of homecoming, "Softly and tenderly Jesus is calling, Calling for you and for me . . . Come home." My brother followed me, though I don't remember being especially aware of his being there. We were asked for our confessions, standing in front of the congregation. "Do you believe that Jesus Christ is the Son of God?" "I do." We were led into a classroom behind the pulpit, where my dad and uncle dressed us in white baptismal robes. Then we were led to the baptistry, a fixture in Churches of Christ. Ours, like many others in the South, was decorated with a primitive painting of a river and sunset, probably emblematic of the Jordan River, though it always reminded me of the White River which ran through my hometown. The preacher placed his right hand on the small of my back, his left hand holding a handkerchief over my nose and mouth, and he leaned me backwards into the cold water . . . .

For years the dead man I left in that baptistry haunted me. He grew up. I pretended not to know him when he showed up at parties or in dreams. But he refused to die. The summer I turned twenty-nine, he told me his name was David. I stopped running away from him. I held him in my arms.

Falling in love with the dying is not easy, though I suppose in some way, we all are. My first love was positive. We would talk about our hometowns, our families, our memories of growing up, aliens in a familiar land. He placed his hand in the small of my back. In my sleep, now that I have given my sexuality a name, I exchange my fears for fantasies, dreaming of the prodigal son's father, his open arms full of grace, imagining the hateful brother, ever mindful of appearances and the improprieties of love. *"My son who was dead is alive again."* How can one predict the plot of exile and reconciliation? How did he tell them where he had come from, where he was going?

THE SUMMER I TURNED twenty-nine, I went to England to study poetry. I did not go to fall in love or to find myself. I went to learn more about an obscure turn-of-the-century poet named Charlotte Mew. She was a woman who refused to choose. A repressed lesbian—though I know "lesbian" is a historically inaccurate term in early modernist England—she never fully accepted or acted upon her sexual desires. A devoted church-goer with a passion for nuns and other figures religious, she would never convert or confirm herself within a church. A poet, she textually inscribed her persona as male, socially marginal, romantically obsessed, and often unstable—madmen, fairy children, farmers, a man going out of his head at the burial of his lover. She took care of an invalid mother and dying sister, and after their deaths, she killed herself.

While I was in London, I decided to visit her grave, at Hampstead Cemetery, just west of Hampstead Heath. I visited the cemetery once, but found it was unattended. It was far too big to simply wander through, entering the circles of each era, like a Dante without a Virgil, hoping to chance upon Mew's grave. So I called a county cemetery authority, who arranged to be in the grounds' office for my visit. He found her plot in the records, next to her sister's, and drew general directions for me on a cemetery map. Mew bought two plots when her sister died in 1927 and arranged to be buried beside her before she killed herself in 1928.

The map led me to a slightly overgrown Victorian section of the cemetery. There, over her sister's grave, was a gravestone. Mew's grave was unmarked, her name an addendum to her sister's stone, followed by the epitaph she chose, "Cast down the seed of weeping and attend" (the words of Beatrice at the entrance to Paradise). Although she spoke thus from her sister's tomb, her final resting place was a bare spot in the line of crosses and stones, an absence, history's invisible daughter. At the foot of her grave grew a blackberry bush, pendulous and prickly. I pulled several berries, kneeling beside the grave, ate them, the grit in my teeth, the juice warm and sweetly sour, like a name on my tongue, like the sting of memory. The air smelled of wet earth and rain, of whom we could have been. Far from home, I took her into my mouth, so I could remember, and so I could speak.

THERE IS ALWAYS A child left behind, or the face of a distant friend translated into a voice. When the telephone rings, there is a face, a memory, a place, a voice that calls us into relation, into the community of long distance. When my mother called to tell me about the death of Paul, it was the simultaneous transmission of his homosexuality and his death, and what was left unsaid—his lack of place in our community. Because of AIDS, I suppose the cultural mingling of the images of homosexuality and death was unavoidable at the time. But that, in itself, is not the point of the story, it is not why I found myself telling it, over and over again. The point of the story is about being left out, about being the invisible son. It is a story about how we remember and how we love. And more than anything else, it is the story of a call from home.

☙

Acknowledgments

I am deeply grateful to David Hooks for beginning this project with me and for working on it steadfastly until he fell ill. And, while I am thankful for his full recovery, it has been with a certain sadness that I have continued as editor of *Crooked Letter i* without him. As former Southerners, we shared such joy and excitement as pieces arrived in response to our calls and ads for essays addressing the coming out experience in the South. The cooperative decision-making we engaged in as we reviewed and edited accepted pieces deepened our friendship. The whoops of joy when a query garnered interest, and the shared disappointment when the inevitable rejections came in, made the process less intimidating. This collection is greatly strengthened by David's participation.

I am indebted to NewSouth Books for taking this book under their wings and presenting it to the public. Thank you, Suzanne La Rosa, Randall Williams, and Brian Seidman for all that you have given and will continue to give to make these voices heard.

Deep gratitude to those who read the manuscript and provided statements of support, and to Dorothy Allison for reading these narratives and sharing her own deeply moving experience as a foreword for the collection. To the writers included in this collection, I bow to your courage in life and in love. Thank you for so generously and beautifully sharing your stories—each a beacon lighting the darkness. And, to my partner, E. Shawn de Jong, gratitude for all that you are.

— C. G.